Nicknames

Nicknames

Tales from the Shallow End of the Manhattan Dating Pool

Mary Geneva
with Lisa Canfield

Mill City Press, Minneapolis

Mill City Press, Inc.
322 First Avenue N, 5th floor
Minneapolis, MN 55401
612.455.2293
www.millcitypublishing.com

Disclaimer:
The opinions expressed in this little book are the author's alone and do not necessarily reflect those of the general female population of Manhattan. The stories are based on her memories of real-life dating experiences. All names and most identifying details have been changed (to protect the guilty). Any resemblance between any of the horrible (or even halfway-decent) guys in this book and any real person is purely coincidental.

ISBN-13: 978-1-63413-215-2
LCCN: 2014921872

Cover Design by www.CosmeCreative.com
Typeset by Mary Kristin Ross

Printed in the United States of America

Dedication

This book is dedicated to the memory of my beloved Dad, who the angels took while I was still writing it. He showed me what a good guy really is, and I hope to one day meet someone who is as kind, selfless, and hardworking as he was.

I also dedicate Nicknames to my girlfriends Zoe, Rose, Fiona, and Amber—especially Zoe, who was with me on the beach in Long Beach, Long Island, on one of our escapes out of the hot, sticky summer in the city when the idea for Nicknames was born. All four of these ladies are my rocks. Without them and their support, this book could not have come to fruition.

Contents

Introduction

The Birth of the Nickname

When most of the world thinks about dating in New York City, they think it's like those images they remember from romantic comedies. You know, the snowy walks through Central Park. The meet-cutes in funky coffee shops. The moonlit kisses framed by the Brooklyn Bridge.

Well, as a real, live, New York single girl, I'm here to set the record straight. Dating in New York is many things—crazy, exasperating, occasionally hilarious—but romantic is not usually one of them.

In New York City, there are 1.07 women for every straight man. That might sound like almost even odds, but when you multiply that by the 1.6 or so million people who live in Manhattan, that difference looks a lot bigger. That is why just scoring a half-hour meet-for-coffee with a member of the opposite sex can be a major accomplishment.

I'm in my thirties and I still haven't experienced my moonlit kiss under the Brooklyn Bridge. Although, I think I remember being groped under the Queensboro Bridge by a drunken cop on St. Paddy's Day.

No, that doesn't count.

The thing is, I came here with those same stars in my eyes that everybody else has when they think about New York City. I grew up on Long Island, which may be a short train ride away, but it's also a whole other world. When my besties and I finally made the leap from Long Island University-CW Post to the bright lights of Manhattan, we all expected our love lives to improve along with our zip codes.

Then again, my zip code might have been my first mistake. I rented my very own Manhattan apartment in the famous neighborhood called Hell's Kitchen: The 'hood of choice for Manhattan's very large population of boys who like boys.

That's right. I'm residing in the village of the Village People.

But giving up hope just isn't my style. I got a dog, but I found out he was using me to meet other dogs (thank you, Rodney Dangerfield). I agreed to a set-up with one of the locals, and he showed up sporting a turquoise "murse" (that's a man-purse, for those of you who have never had the pleasure of sharing a meal with a man whose bag is nicer than yours) and more skincare tips than the beauty issue of Cosmo.

I made the best of it. I have to say, my complexion has never looked better.

Please, don't ask me about meeting guys at work, like every Facebook friend or relative I've ever had. I work with elderly people who are determined to enter their eternal slumber in the city that never sleeps. The average guy I meet at work is about 80. Even their kids are too old for me.

And the grandkids? I may have met one or two on a dating website.

Like so many millions of my sisters-in-singlehood, I have turned to what must be the planet's fastest-growing industry: The wacky world of online dating. It's really a genius idea, shopping for the perfect date just like you shop for a new floor lamp on Amazon—just click on your preferences (How tall? How bright? Modern or traditional?) and they'll show you a list of men to match, ready to go.

Except, when your "package" finally shows up, it looks nothing (not to mention acts nothing) like the picture that made you pull out your Visa in the first place.

For me, the key to staying sane has been my girlfriends. Lucky for me, they're all going through their own personal versions of Manhattan dating hell. Not that we haven't had fun along the way.

The three of us have probably logged hundreds of dates between us. As girlfriends do, we discuss those dates regularly, down to the tiniest detail.

That's where the whole nickname thing got started. I can't pinpoint the exact moment (or the exact guy out of our long list of duds) that started it all, but once it caught on, the nickname thing seemed to take on a life of its own. Right around the moment a relationship would start to die, a nickname for the poor bastard who was about to get the axe would be born, falling out of the mouth of the gal whose Facebook status was about to switch back to "single." So Joe became Sloppy Joe, Nick turned into Small Dick, John became Insufficient Funds, Rob turned into OnStar. The list goes on and on. Even if the nickname-giver was still holding out hope that the guy might actually be a keeper, the nickname was always the deciding factor. Once it had been bestowed, that was it.

Done. Finito. So long, Charlie.

It's not about being mean, I swear. It's about finding the silver lining, which, more often than not, is the ability to laugh at the sheer volume and variety of bad dates we've been subjected to.

That, my friends, is what brings me to this book.

I can't make this shit up. So I might as well share it.

One

Till Death (or a Turkish Invasion) Do Us Part

Unlike a lot of women in their thirties, I'm in no personal rush to put a ring on it—or have one put on me. I've been there and done that—a long time ago.

Therefore, the next time, I want to be as sure as humanly possible that I'm not going to screw it up. Possibly by waiting until the endorphins settle down before I walk down the aisle for a second time.

Of course, I don't want to be too hard on myself, because I was only twenty-one the first (and so far only) time I tied the knot. I really had no idea what I was getting into.

My life at the time wasn't exactly stable. It was my sophomore year at CW Post, and I came home to live with my dad and stepmom after spending a semester in London. While I was away, my sister moved in. Suddenly, I felt like there was no place for me.

That's when Burak swept in.

If I had a "type," I guess it would be tall, dark, and foreign. Blame it on my time in London. I know, when you think of England, you probably think of pale and pasty British guys. But no! London offered a whole range of international manly delights a girl from the 'burbs could never even imagine.

So when I got home after my London adventure and wound up bored and alone and feeling unwelcome in my own home, I was ripe and ready to be rescued. No white horse required—just a foreign passport.

Of course, I was stuck on Long Island, which isn't known for its cosmopolitan flair. How was I ever going to find the exotic man of my dreams? I definitely wasn't going to meet him at the local Red Lobster.

So, I went looking on the Internet. There was this new thing at the time called online dating. I had no idea at the time that it would end up generating much of my romantic life.

I logged on—and I met Burak.

Burak was your typical charmer—exactly the tall, dark, sexy foreigner I had pictured in my fantasies. He was from Istanbul, Turkey, from a good, well-to-do family (something that sounded mighty appealing to me at the time) and he was getting his master's in chemistry at Hofstra University, which just happened to be located minutes away from CW Post!

I was smitten pretty much from the get-go. I remember rushing from class back to my dorm room to chat with him every single day. It was so exciting! Plus, he could type a lot better than he could speak English. The first time we talked on the phone, my heart was pounding the whole time, knowing that there was this exotic, mysterious guy on the other end, and he liked me! It didn't matter that the conversation basically consisted of one-line sentences and trying to figure out what the other person was saying. He seemed so much more mature and together than the sloppy American frat boys I usually met.

Eventually, we arranged to meet in person at a local bar. He brought a friend to do a lot of the translating, but that just made it even more exciting. I didn't care if his English sucked! I knew it was bound to improve, which it rapidly did. Besides, the language of love knows no boundaries.

At least, the language of sex doesn't.

The chemistry between us was explosive. I had never experienced anything like it with anyone else. But it wasn't just about the sex (the mind-blowing, amazing sex). We became inseparable really fast. I felt like I would be lost without him. With all the crazy shit going on in my dysfunctional family, he was my rock. He had become my lover, boyfriend, and best friend in only a few months.

After about four months, the semester was drawing to a close, and there we were on a starry night, sitting in the oh-so-romantic location of the local Chili's parking lot. I "innocently" asked Burak what his plans for the future were.

He told me he planned to return to the "motherland."

I burst into tears.

The next week, we went to dinner at a Turkish restaurant in the city, where Burak proposed a solution. Well, actually, he proposed. He asked for my hand in marriage, but he was so awkward I didn't realize he was serious. At least, not at first.

As the end of the semester drew closer, I realized he actually wanted to marry me! The closer to his graduation we got, the better the idea sounded.

Okay, I was twenty-one and had no idea if being married would really work.

On the other hand, he needed a green card to stay in the USA legally.

And we were in love. At least we thought we were in love, thanks to all the endorphins that were bouncing around our brains and making our bodies tingle.

I decided to go for it.

I still had my standards, however. If we were going to get married, I needed a proper proposal. So we drove around Nautical Mile, this lovely shopping and dining area perched right on the water. Burak found the ideal spot, dropped to one knee, and asked me to be his wife. Of course, I said yes, and he pulled out this gorgeous ring and slipped it on my finger. It wasn't an engagement ring (I didn't want anyone to know I was getting married so soon), but a "promise" ring—the promise was that he would give me my big white wedding "someday" after we eloped at City Hall.

I still wear that ring every day. It's not that I'm still in love with him, but the ring is beautiful, and it will always mean a lot to me. Plus, it's a great story to tell my kids some-day: "Your mother eloped with a foreign guy four months after meeting him—yes, it was very exciting and sexy, but maybe make sure your potential spouse speaks English before you take the plunge!"

I took my best friend and designated witness, Fiona, with me to pick out a dress for the ceremony. Luckily, my part-time job was as the cosmetics girl at the Estee Lauder counter at the local mall. That meant I had an employee discount—hey, I was a college girl on a budget! I pulled a dress off the rack and got ready for my "big day."

A few days later, Fiona, Burak, his best friend, and I

met up at City Hall. It all seemed so surreal. Was I really going to go through with this?

When the judge started reading the vows, I got this feeling in the pit of my stomach. It was as though I knew what I was doing was wrong. That it would not end well. That I had long passed the point where I could stop it.

And I just burst out laughing.

It's not the first time—it's a nervous reaction I've had all my life. Then again, I probably wasn't the first person to laugh through their City Hall wedding, and I wouldn't be the last. We were just two crazy kids from opposite sides of the globe "in love." What could possibly go wrong? Isn't life supposed to be spontaneous and fun?

That first year *was* fun—incredibly fun. Our marriage was a complete secret. Only Fiona knew the truth. I kept living on campus until I graduated, passing Burak off as my "boyfriend." I even had the pledges in my sorority perform for him at his birthday party. No one knew my tall, dark, sexy boyfriend was actually my husband.

After I graduated, we moved into a nice apartment just thirty-five minutes east of the city together. Burak left his job as a pizza delivery boy and bought his own business: A women's shoe store that I helped him name. My feet never looked so good! Then he took me home to Turkey to meet his entire family, which was my first trip there.

It was as though he was making me part of the family.

Burak's family lived right on the Bosporus, this beautiful waterway that runs through Istanbul. It divides the city in half: one side is in Europe and the other is in Asia, which was just incredibly cool. Not many other cities span two continents. His family's neighborhood was like something out of a storybook. It was old and quaint, with narrow, winding streets. The houses, which were more like apartment buildings, sat perched on top of the hills overlooking the water.

Everyone in the village knew everyone else. And Burak's family lived all together in one of the apartment buildings with one aunt and uncle on the first floor; another aunt, uncle, and cousins on the second; and his parents and brother up on top. It felt warm and loving, like a real family—everything I never had growing up.

The highlight of the whole trip was the "ring ceremony," which I guess is the Turkish version of an engagement. It was held at the cafe across the street, which was owned by the neighbors and attached to their house. I was surrounded by Turkish people, so I couldn't understand what anyone was saying. Nevertheless, I felt welcomed into Burak's family and culture with open arms.

The ceremony was beautiful. Burak and I wore rings that were attached with a red ribbon. Then we cut the ribbon together and all of his family and friends and the villagers cheered and started dancing around us.

It was magical.

I had never felt so welcomed and wanted in my life. In case that wasn't incredible enough, we finished off the evening yachting around the beautiful city, the lights twinkling all around us. I guess that is even more romantic than a kiss under the Brooklyn Bridge.

As amazing as that trip was, my return to Turkey a year and a half later for my long-dreamed-of, big, white wedding was an even bigger deal.

Once again, Fiona was my maid of honor, which

meant she was on dress duty again. This was no off-the-rack special this time; this was a real wedding dress. Amazingly, the very first one I tried on was "the one." We both knew it instantly. Fiona's mother made my veil by hand, which meant so much to me. I chose gorgeous blue dresses for my four bridesmaids. The most important piece, which I chose to tie it all together with, was my bouquet.

For years, I had dreamed of carrying a bouquet of red roses with a pearl inside each one. I had been talking to Burak about it forever—the whole time we were planning the wedding—and I even found a florist in Turkey who would create this dream bouquet for me. The plan was that Burak would pick up the bouquet the night before the ceremony.

He forgot.

I don't know if he was just so swept up in all the excitement and all the family or what, but he had to know how important this bouquet was to me. I had only reminded him at least 100 times. Therefore, the day of our wedding was somewhat stressful, especially because my bouquet didn't arrive until half an hour before the ceremony.

But, it showed up, and everything else was going perfectly. My father, may he rest in peace, my sister, my friends, and everyone I loved made the trip to Turkey and was there by my side.

The wedding itself was the stuff of legends. Like something right out of *My Big Fat Greek Wedding*, but more elegant and less, well, big and fat. The celebration was at a beautiful venue outside on the water. It seemed the entire village turned out for the occasion.

It was more than a wedding. It was a production. It started with my entrance—my bridesmaids and I arrived at the ceremony via a luxury yacht owned by Burak's friend Ahmed.

Ahmed is a story in itself. He had started getting hot and heavy with my bridesmaid Zoe, and somehow ended up taking all my girls rug shopping at the Grand Bazaar in Istanbul. At some point during the mandatory price haggling, he decided to drive a hard bargain by pulling out a gun and waving it the face of the rug shop owner!

Let's just say my girls got very good prices on floor coverings.

But I digress. Back at the ceremony, I stepped off the yacht, and my dad was there to greet me. My girls walked down the aisle in their beautiful blue dresses, then my dad took my arm and we followed. It was utterly enchanting.

Except for this one weird thing.

This wasn't an ordinary wedding, and one of the "unique" aspects was that we didn't want ordinary music. Instead of marching down the aisle to "Here Comes the Bride" or "The Four Seasons" or any of the typical music you usually hear at weddings, I walked down the aisle to a song Burak had chosen especially for me. It was a Moby song called "Porcelain."

The song starts with his dreams of death, moves into him (accidentally) lying to and hurting his partner, and wraps up with him ending the relationship and asking his partner to confess to never having wanted him in the first place.

Romantic, right?

Okay, so maybe Burak's English still wasn't up to par. Maybe he just really, really liked the song.

Or, maybe it was a sign.

Honestly, I didn't notice. I was swept up in how perfect, romantic, and glamorous the whole thing was. When my father and I reached the end of the aisle, Burak and I were seated together at a long table with gorgeous linens and the magnificent Istanbul skyline behind us. Then a man, who I assume was the village judge, stood and said some things in Turkish. (I can't be sure, I was just trying to learn the language on the plane ride over.) I just said yes (or "evet" in Turkish) and hoped it was the right answer. Then my friend Crystal read some vows I wrote in English, and Burak and I signed our names in the big huge book that I assume was the wedding register. I threw my beautiful rose bouquet into the water and that was it. The deal was sealed.

According to Turkish law, we were legally man and wife.

At that moment, fireworks went off behind us. I didn't even realize they were part of the ceremony. Burak and his family had planned the entire wedding. It was as if we were in a fairytale.

The reception was equally beautiful. I made the rounds with my "new" husband, thanking each guest for coming. As is Turkish custom, each guest placed gold jewelry or coins in a special silk bag when I greeted them, which is a lovely tradition, but after two hours, I started getting tired. And hungry. Moreover, I sort of felt as though I were trick or treating for lira (Turkish currency).

All I really wanted was a good stiff drink. To my shock, Burak said I couldn't have one. He insisted I stay completely sober so that I could "appropriately" entertain our guests.

No drinks at my own wedding? Seriously?

Looking back, that definitely should have been a red

flag. The second, at least, after "Porcelain." It was a party, however, and it was beautiful, and my bridesmaids snuck me drinks in the bathroom, which was kind of naughty and fun. Because I didn't get a chance to eat one bite of food at my own wedding, after starving myself down twenty pounds (the skinniest I've ever been in my life) to fit into my dress, those few drinks in the bathroom were more than enough.

The next day we left on our honeymoon. We went to Bodrum, which is this absolutely gorgeous European vacation resort in southern Turkey.

When I say we, I don't just mean my "new" husband and me.

I mean his entire family.

Apparently, the clan I had married into traveled in packs. Burak's brother, cousins, and friends all made the trip to Bodrum with us. Not only that, but the men stayed together almost 24/7, hanging out during every waking hour.

As a result, I barely saw my husband all week. That was not what I expected from my long-awaited honeymoon. When I complained and asked Burak to maybe spend some of the time with me, he got mad and snapped back at me that I just had a beautiful wedding and that should have been enough.

It wasn't much of a honeymoon. We only had sex once.

I hoped things would get better when we went home to Long Island and got back to our normal lives, but that's when things really started to get weird.

Burak's family followed us home.

Apparently, when I signed my name in that big book, I was not just legally marrying Burak, but all of his relatives as well. Soon, the pack began to migrate to eastern shores. First, it was just his brother. Then, his parents. Whoever came had never heard of a hotel room—they all camped out in our little two-bedroom apartment.

These bonds of matrimony weren't limited to family, either. It seemed like anyone with a Turkish passport and some connection to my new husband was welcome to crash at our pad. Unfortunately, this included one friend who used to lock himself in our small guest room, smoking cigarette after cigarette and banging his 30-years-younger assistant. This made it especially difficult to put my smiley face on and pretend I didn't know anything during our many dinners with his wife and children.

Yikes!

Meanwhile, Burak threw himself into his business, to the point that he started traveling a lot. Meaning, I was left alone, sometimes for days on end. Or, I wouldn't be alone, because his parents would be staying in our apartment for one of their two- or three-month-long visits. Then I had company—but it wasn't the kind of company I wanted.

Through it all, I worked full time. I would come home tired and depressed, with no husband to greet me, and plop down on the couch and not want to move. Burak's mom, who was constantly smiling and spoke zero English, would put her hand on my head and say something in Turkish. She was incredibly sweet—she was a housewife that cooked amazing Turkish food from sunup to sundown (something I still miss to this day). In fact, both of his parents were awesome people.

But this wasn't the life I signed up for.

Things with Burak kept changing—and not for the

better. When we were first together, he always spoke English and made sure he included me in the conversation. As time went on, he just spoke Turkish when his friends were around, so I was completely cut out of the discussion.

There were times when we could go a whole week without really talking.

If I dared to ask where he was or tell him I missed him that just made things worse. He'd tune me out at home and stay away for even longer on his trips. He did manage to communicate that he still expected me to have breakfast on the table at 6:00 a.m., however. I had no problem cooking if he just appeared on a semi-regular basis.

But that didn't happen.

I thought adopting an animal would make me less lonely. Burak agreed to a cat—but only if it was a Turkish cat, which I did manage to find through the local rescue group. Sadly, a thousand lint rollers later, I realized Diva wasn't going to fix my marriage.

After a year, Burak was well on his way to building an international shoe business (with my support!) and was spending more and more time away. His homecoming routine had become:

1. Putting his headphones on as soon as he walked in
2. Turning on a Turkish movie
3. Tuning me out.

I was miserable.

I was only twenty-four years old, and I was crying myself to sleep almost every night. Honestly, it had been going on pretty much since we got back from our big, beautiful, perfect wedding. I couldn't believe the same Burak I fell in love with was treating me like a piece of furniture. How could things be so different after all the passion and romance we had at the beginning? Maybe cultural differences were to blame, but at that point, I really didn't care. I wanted to be treated like a person!

On our fourth Thanksgiving, one of Burak's friends invited us to a holiday gathering at his mosque in New Jersey. This was not my first time in a mosque—I respected Burak's culture because I loved him, and I like to think of myself as open-minded. I went to weddings and holidays in the mosque. I even took my shoes off and wore one of those "babushkas" my friends and I called the Muslim head wrap when I was inside.

This day was a little different.

The T-Day gathering itself was nice—a lot of people, a ton of food, and music. Nevertheless, I felt uncomfortable. I noticed how the men all hung out with the men smoking cigars, while the women all stayed with the women in the kitchen. This was not my idea of a good time. But when I tried to sit next to Burak, he would shoo me back to the kitchen with the rest of the women.

Open-minded or not, I couldn't accept the message that I was "beneath" my husband. This was 21st century America, for God's sake!

Then again, it didn't really matter whom I was hanging out with, because no one, male or female, made any attempt to talk to me. At least not in English.

So yeah, I was in kind of a shitty mood and not feeling particularly thankful that Thanksgiving. My thoughts must have shown on my face—I must have looked mean, or angry, or like some kind of Muslim-hater—because that night, Burak chewed me out.

It was the start of a very un-merry holiday season. By the

time Christmas rolled around, it was obvious our relationship was nose-diving into the great abyss. Burak had promised to decorate the Christmas tree with me—I felt like he was the only family I had since my dad married my crazy stepmother—but he didn't show up. That's when it hit me like a ton of bricks.

It was over.

A few days later, we sat down for "the talk." We agreed that our marriage wasn't going to go the distance. Since we were young and just starting out, we decided to do the responsible thing and keep living together and support each other financially until we could go our separate ways.

We stuck to the bargain for a while, but all awkward, painful things must come to an end. Eventually I reached my breaking point and all hell broke loose. Burak hadn't been home—let alone given me any sort of sign he was even alive—for three days. I waited and waited and waited, until I finally called him and screamed, "Pack up your shit and get out!"

I couldn't believe those words came out of my mouth. I had no clue how I was going to survive on my own. I didn't know if I could make a car payment, let alone take care of myself, but I knew he had to go.

Burak came home that night with his brother, who held several, large, industrial-sized garbage bags, and they loaded all his worldly possessions into them.

We sat on the couch and cried together. Then, as if it never happened, he was gone.

Yes, it was sad. Just writing this story, I feel sad. However, I was also hopeful. After spending almost three years of my life crying and depressed, I had a chance to start over, instead of spending another fifty years in married misery. I was only twenty-five. I still had my whole life ahead of me.

The only thing left was to make it legal. In order to expedite the proceedings and minimize the cost factor, we agreed to share a lawyer—one we saw advertised on Queens Boulevard. Less than $800 later, we were divorced.

Then, almost without taking a breath, Burak married someone else and divorced her within a year. Leaving her with a baby!

Burak would later tell me that he made a big mistake divorcing me, that his parents missed me, that if we'd only had a baby together our marriage would have been saved.

Oh, God. Creating spawn with him would have been a life sentence.

Sometimes I feel bad when he says he still shows people our wedding video and brags that we had the best wedding out of all of his friends. He also still claims he's going to buy me that Benz he promised me when his business makes it big. I'm still waiting, but I did get custody of the cat.

So... What did I learn from getting married at the ripe young age of twenty-one?

- Look before you leap. Don't confuse the tingles of a new relationship with "true love." (This applies at any age.)

- Both women and men deserve to be treated with respect.

- Adopting an animal or making a baby will not save your marriage.

- If your groom picks a wedding song with the lyrics "this is goodbye," it just might be.

Two

Everybody Back in the Pool!

After the Burak debacle, I spent some time licking my wounds and trying to recover. Being treated the way Burak had treated me did some real damage to my self-esteem—and seeing someone who had been head over heels in love with me slowly come to regard me as something like a piece of furniture that also cooked breakfast kind of shattered my faith in the whole man-woman thing.

Overall, it took me about a year to regain enough confidence and guts to stick a toe back in the dating pool.

Let's just say those early attempts did not go well.

It was crazy. I was only twenty-five. I had been on plenty of dates in my life. I had even been married, for God's sake. At one point in my life, I knew how to act around men, but for some reason, the whole Burak situation had reduced me to some kind of babbling idiot. Maybe it was all those long months of having no one to talk to while Burak traveled and communicated only in Turkish.

The bottom line? I no longer knew how to communicate with members of the opposite sex, let alone socialize with them. In fact, I was scaring guys away.

My "coming out" happened at a big party. My friend was involved with a fundraiser for a local ambulance company and, despite my newfound lack of social skills, I actually managed to meet three guys there. Probably because I was so nervous, I got very, very drunk. In my drunken state, I gave three lucky young men my phone number (and possibly more who had the good sense not to call me).

This probably was not such a good idea. The first guy made the mistake of asking me out for ice cream. Sounds like a simple enough request, right? A casual date, no big commitment like dinner or a movie, no alcohol to loosen the inhibitions. And, hey, everyone likes ice cream, right?

So how did I respond? I completely freaked out. I had no concept of what to say to this guy. I babbled as if I had completely lost my command of the English language. He may as well have been asking me to join him for a three-some, or to help him move, or to quit my job and move to Tibet. A basic ice cream date was apparently too much for me to handle.

Then the second guy called me. For some reason, that little switch in my brain that had once enabled me to carry on a coherent conversation with a member of the opposite sex switched off again. This time, I called the guy by the wrong name.

But hey, bright side: At least I didn't call him Burak.

I was no better when the third guy picked up the phone and entered the dangerous waters known as trying to date a divorcée. I got the name right, but after that I completely lost the ability to carry on a phone conversation.

I tried, I really did, but I couldn't manage to come up with anything beyond the kind of simple, three-word sentences you learn in kindergarten. "How are you?" "I am fine." At least I didn't say, "I want cookie." At least I hope I didn't.

Beyond that, there was a lot of silence. You know those long, painful pauses in a conversation when you wait for someone to say something, and no one does? A lot of that happened. I had absolutely no idea what to say to him.

Five years with Burak had turned me into the dating equivalent of a five-year-old. It would take me two long years to get my groove back.

What did I learn from my first post-divorce dating experiences?

- Healing takes time—sometimes longer than you might like or expect.

- Dating is NOT like riding a bike. If you stop for a long period of time, you can forget how.

- Charity events are a great place to meet men. If you happen to be invited to one, brush up on your conversation skills beforehand.

Three
Early Adventures

Of course, Burak wasn't the first man I ever dated—even if, for a while, it seemed like he might be the last. High school and my pre-Burak college years were prime dating years for me. In fact, the nickname thing actually started before I met my ex-husband.

Giorgio

Giorgio was the first man I ever loved and one of the few guys to cross my path to escape the shame of the nickname. I was seventeen when we met, and he was just the kind of bad boy who makes girls' hearts melt. He still is—he runs with a bad crowd and seems to attract trouble.

As in, spending some time in prison trouble.

He emailed me from prison to tell me:

1. He was working out every day.

2. He was growing his hair in.

3. The food was shit.

Back when we were dating, Giorgio's tendency to attract trouble wasn't the problem. Long Island was.

No offense to Long Island—many people besides me think of it as their hometown, from Jerry Seinfeld to Mariah Carey.

The thing about Jerry and Mariah and me is, we left. Giorgio didn't. And I don't think he ever will.

A lot of people who live out on Long Island—particularly in my hometown located in Suffolk County, which I refer to as the east-ass end—don't know and/or don't care that there's a whole big world out there waiting to be discovered. Not to mention the fact that The Greatest City in the World is just a short train ride away.

In just an hour, you can be in the center of the universe. But, as a Suffolk County denizen might say, so freakin' what?

Suffolk people—I guess I can call them Suf-folks!—are stubbornly, proudly, and pretty much permanently stuck in their own little bubbles. They grow up in Suffolk, they go to school in Suffolk, they get jobs in Suffolk, they have families in Suffolk—a practice that usually includes making the babies before getting married—and many die in Suffolk. Unless they were fortunate enough to be born into a rich family that owned a house out in the Hamptons and a pad in the city, which I definitely was not.

In fact, after my parents split when I was seven, I was reared on a steady diet of powdered milk and government cheese. Scrumptious… Not! Although, I managed to make some pretty creative meals out of the ingredients that came from those white-labeled cans. Even more importantly, at an early age, some internal survival instinct kicked in and I decided that was not the life I was destined to live.

Maybe I'm still a little raw around the edges from my own personal "Scruffolk" experiences, but I knew I wanted something different. I wanted adventure. I wanted to live life to the fullest. Which is part of the reason why Giorgio and I, while we're still good friends, are nothing more than that.

Giorgio lives the classic Suffolk County life. Before he went to prison, he worked in plumbing and lived with his wife, also a Suffolk County lifer, and her three kids. That is why I wasn't allowed to call or text him after 4:30pm. Yeah, we're just friends, but he still thinks she'll go stark raving batshit if she sees a text from another woman.

Before he was locked up, Giorgio and I would see each other fairly regularly. He was working at a construction site just down the block from where I live (which means he has some awareness of Manhattan!). So on Mondays, when I had the day off, Giorgio and I would get together for lunch. He would hold on to every minute of this half-hour lunch break together as if it were our last thirty minutes on earth.

Of course, this could be due to the fact that Giorgio still thinks we're going to get married one day.

Yes, to each other.

From time to time, he would tell me he was still in love with me. He still does, through CorrLinks email—the email system designed to allow prison inmates to communicate with the outside world. Sometimes, he'll tell me how he wants his life to be better when he gets out, that he doesn't want to be stuck in Suffolk forever. He even tells me how much his family still misses me and talks about me—a recurring theme in my life.

Why am I always the one who got away—from the wrong guy?

By now, you're probably thinking, "Jeez, does this girl ever lighten up? I thought this was supposed to be funny!" I promise, not every guy in this book ends up crying over the spilled milk that was me.

In fact, Giorgio and Burak are pretty much the only two.

The vast majority of my dating stories tend to be more like this one.

Dildo Boy

Yes, the nickname of this particular date is Dildo Boy—a clear sign that there will be no tears or regrets or anything remotely depressing in this story!

Dildo Boy—we'll call him DB from now on—is a guy I dated in college. Unlike most guys I date, both then and now, we actually made it to the third date. We all know what's supposed to happen on the third date, right?

I brought DB back to my college suite, where my roomies were parked in the living room, smoking what must have been several ounces—maybe pounds—of pot. These girls were out of their minds. So out of their minds that when I introduced my date (by his name, which I have since forgotten) they threw a dildo at him!

Classy, I know. At least it wasn't my dildo!

They claimed they were playing a game called "Pass the Dildo," but, despite the nickname that has lasted for well over a decade, DB wasn't playin'. He lasted about five minutes, then made some lame excuse about having to pick up a friend and booked it the hell out of there.

Sadly, that was the end for DB and me. There was never a date number four. In fact, I never saw the guy again. However, one of my former roomies spotted him at a party three years later. He was still too embarrassed to say a word. Imagine how embarrassed he'd be if he knew he was being referred to as Dildo Boy!

Hoover

If you've ever been a sorority girl, you already know formal night is the biggest night of the college calendar year. If you happened to miss the joys of non-biological sisterhood, picture your senior prom in high school, but add in that there are no adults "chaperoning," you don't have to worry about your parents, and at least some of your friends are over twenty-one and have access to as much alcohol (and other stuff) as you want.

In other words, it's like the prom, only X-rated.

This brings me to Hoover. He was my date to the formal one year, and the evening went so well that we decided to prolong the magic by returning to my room.

This was a decision I would soon regret. While this was only our first date (the third date rule doesn't apply to formal night), we quickly made it to third base. That's when things got intensely strange and the evening devolved into one of the most painful sexual encounters of my life.

Hoover became Hoover because it felt like I was being vacuumed.

Yes, I know that sounds disgusting. It *was* disgusting! But, it's also another early example of the nicknaming phenomenon in action. The next day, when I shared my story with my sorority sisters, he was christened

"Hoover." Unbeknownst to him, we have called him Hoover ever since.

I hope his future girlfriends have a high threshold for pain!

The Two Roberts

This isn't exactly a pre-Burak story, although I did meet one of the players in high school. His name was Robert, but for the purposes of this story, we'll call him Robert #1. If you've been paying attention, you know the fact that I knew Robert #1 in high school means he was another Long Islander like Giorgio, and likely not destined for the long haul in my romantic life.

However, Robert #1 was, and still is, a firefighter. Come on, what red-blooded American girl doesn't have a thing for firefighters?

When Robert and I reconnected about ten years later on Facebook, I had no problem meeting him for a drink one evening after work. And then a few more times for dinner and drinks. We did seem to have some chemistry going. In firefighter parlance, you could say sparks were flying.

So a few weeks later, we were sitting at a bar when the girl on the stool to my left decided to interject herself into our date. We learned that her name was Reyna, that she was 25, that she had moved to the Upper West Side from Mississippi two years earlier, and that she was clearly a little nuts. Why else would she be sitting alone at a bar chatting up a couple that was clearly on a date?

Well, apparently there was another reason. This strange, somewhat despondent creature told us she had met a guy at that very same bar the night before, and had convinced him to return to meet her there that night.

Of course, this didn't stop her from overtly flirting with Robert #1.

In between batting her eyelashes at my date, she peppered me with questions, mostly along the lines of "Do I seem needy?" and "Does this sound desperate?"

(Answer: yes, and YES!)

Amazingly, the guy showed up. And guess what? He was named Robert! We'll call him Robert #2.

The most amazing thing was the fact that Robert #2 was incredibly good-looking. As in, every-female-head-in-the-room-turns good-looking. He wore a gorgeous suit and looked like he had his shit together. I couldn't help asking the question (in my head, not out loud, of course):

What is this seemingly put together guy doing with a hot mess like Reyna, and why isn't he with me?

Whatever he was doing with her, he wound up doing it with us. As unusual as the circumstances might seem, Reyna and the two Roberts and I hung out, drank, and chatted for a while, until I went outside for a cigarette. Robert #2 also wanted a smoke and joined me, leaving our dates inside. We talked and smoked for a few minutes, then went back inside, settled our bills and the two couples went our separate ways.

Robert #1, being from the 'burbs, had a car and drove me home.

That was that, right? Not exactly.

A couple of days later, the phone rang. I picked it up, and a somewhat familiar male voice on the other end said, "I know this is going to sound weird, but…"

Holy crap. It was Robert #2!

How the hell was he calling me when we hadn't exchanged phone numbers or anything but friendly "having a cigarette outside" conversation?

Apparently, while Robert #2 and I were innocently smoking and chatting outside, Robert #1 and Reyna were not so innocently chatting and exchanging numbers inside. After Robert #1 dropped me off that night, he called Reyna, or Reyna called him, and they went back into the city to hang out together.

If you're still following this twisted tale, you're thinking that still doesn't explain the part where Robert #2 got *my* number.

I do remember that when the four of us were together in the bar, out of the goodness of my heart, I gave poor, lonely Reyna my number in case she ever wanted to hang out. Robert #2 told me *he* found *me* by checking her phone.

I didn't totally buy it. But then again, I didn't care. Robert #2 was gorgeous and successful and a big step up from Robert #1—so I saw it as a win-win. Reyna got my Robert, I got hers, and the rest, while brief, is history.

What did I learn from my Early Adventures?

- To be honest, not a lot—except that my dating life was going to be one hell of a ride!

Four
Love on the Job

As I mentioned at the beginning of this book, one of the major stumbling blocks in my romantic life has been my job. Pretty much everyone I know has had an office romance—after all, who knows you better than the cubicle-mate you see every day, the client who knows exactly how to make you laugh, the supervisor who knows just where your favorite place to go for lunch is?

But for me, spending my days surrounded by 80-year-olds, those options just weren't available.

Not that some of them didn't try...

Mr. M

It was amazing that Mr. M survived long enough to live in what is considered the Ritz Carlton of assisted living facilities. More power to him! He was a major alcoholic, with not much family to speak of and no friends. His time in the community was not long because he was known for peeing in the pool and having three liters of vodka delivered from the local liquor store every three days. After a few weeks, he was asked to leave.

Nevertheless, apparently I made an impression on him. About three weeks after he was dismissed from the building, I received a voicemail from him. He told me that he was in the hospital and not doing well. He wanted to leave me something in his will. I should have called back right away, but I'm the most honest person ever, sometimes a fault of mine, and I felt funny about taking advantage of the poor guy. About a week later, I did call to check on him, but it was too late.

Now, I'm not the kind of girl who would exploit an eighty-year old alcoholic with no family. If he thought I was the only person who cared about him, I feel good knowing I had given him some sort of happiness in his life, however briefly.

But still... What if I had answered my phone that day? I could have been set for life—*if* he was serious and not in a drunken stupor.

Rico Suave

My one other significant office romance happened when I took a break from my work among the aged and took a job where I could interact with people who were too young for Medicare. I worked at the timeshare desk in one of the busiest hotels in New York, where my job consisted of sitting in the lobby and trying to convince guests to sit through a ninety-minute timeshare presentation.

Oh, joy!

This particular hotel was specifically known for hosting major business conferences. That meant one of the perks of the job was being hit on by guys in suits from every part of the globe. Most of them were still too old for me, not to mention married.

Then I saw the man I eventually nicknamed Rico Suave.

I spotted him sitting across the lobby, checking his Blackberry, then looking over at me, then back at the Blackberry. Suddenly he got up and—ohmigod—started walking toward my desk. I felt a lump in my throat as he approached. He was tall, dark, and handsome—my type exactly—and never mind that, I was actually about to be hit on by a guy under the age of fifty!

He came up to me, smiled his million-dollar smile, and I just about melted right there at my desk. He downright *oozed* power, success, and charm.

We chatted for fifteen minutes or so. He told me he was from California—Malibu, to be exact—and in town doing charity work with former heads of state.

In fact, Rico knew everyone who was important and rich. He was the brains behind some software technology company he started in his twenties that ultimately grew into a multi-million dollar business. He was in thirties, and he was a millionaire.

Later on, I Google-stalked him and found out that a few years earlier a magazine had rated him one of the top forty entrepreneurs.

Looking back on our conversation, I realize that he was really laying on the charm, and that half the stuff that came out of his mouth sounded like a load of BS. Nevertheless, I ate it up. I was caught up in the fantasy that out of the millions of people who passed through the lobby where I worked every day, the gods magically sent this one perfect man to me. What can I say? I'm an incurable romantic.

We had our first "date" in Scottsdale. I had flown across the country—my first time in Arizona—to run in a half-marathon for the Leukemia and Lymphoma Society. He flew down for the night to meet me. I was so excited. We hadn't seen each other since he strutted over to my desk in New York.

The feeling lasted for about five minutes. My first realization was that Rico was extremely cocky. Okay, maybe that was just a part of the lifestyle of the rich and famous, but he seemed to be laying the whole "I'm so rich" act on a little thick. First stop was the Ferrari showroom, where he stopped to brag about the shiny new toy he had just purchased to the poor sales clerks, who couldn't exactly get up and leave. To be honest, he sounded like a real douchebag, but I told myself I just wasn't used to "rich person speak" and tried to go with the flow and act like I was comfortable.

Next stop was a jewelry store, where he treated me to a peek at the $50,000 watch he had just purchased. Like I really gave a rat's ass! If you're going to brag about your toys, at least buy *me* something—a rose, a drink, whatever! But it was all about him. When he insisted that I would cum in my pants if I ever rode in his red Ferrari, I threw up in my mouth. More than a little.

He kind of made up for it that night when I got to stay at the Ritz in Paradise Valley instead of the Marriot in town, where the rest of my team was booked. Still, my tall, dark, über-successful Sicilian god (of course he was foreign!) wasn't exactly a macho man in the sack. His moans were—can I say it?—rather, ahem, interesting. Moreover, his demands were just weird—things no straight guy had ever asked me for before.

But, hey, there's a first time for everything, and after all, life is supposed to be interesting and fun. I thought maybe that it was a rich, spoiled, California boy thing. He also had more facial products than any female I have ever met. Jumbo-sized Ziploc bags stuffed to the breaking point with *products!* He told me because he travelled so much, he needed to keep all his stuff in Ziploc bags, especially as he never knew when he would have to make public appearances.

At one point he let me know that he won some sort of award for his charity work. It must be nice being loaded, so you can help save the world instead of trying to sell time-shares to horny businessmen.

We stayed in touch for a year and a half. He usually communicated via three- to four-word text messages: "Miss u kisses." "Miss u so much." And when I was lucky, "Get excited in NY soon."

The New York visits happened a handful of times. He had an office here and I would see him when he came to check in. I always stayed with him in his hotel suite, which was awesome. I also always had to leave first thing in the morning. Despite all his millions, he never once offered to pay for my cab home.

The final time he came to town, I really wanted my best friend Zoe to meet him and give me her opinion. I had always talked him up to her, but I couldn't shake the feeling that something was off about the guy. I knew if anyone could see through someone's BS, it was my girl Zoe.

I made reservations at Lavo, this popular NYC restaurant that turns into a nightclub in the middle of your meal.

Then I told Zoe to make her own reservation at Lavo half an hour before ours so she could just "happen" to meet my "friend." When Rico and I arrived, Zoe and her date actually happened to be seated right next to us! This wouldn't be a passing hello-goodbye thing. She was going to get the full Rico.

The four of us chatted and had a good time for a while, but then things took a turn for the weird. It was Elvis night at Lavo, which Rico found oddly irresistible. He was like a jumping jack on speed, continually jumping in and out of his chair, largely in pursuit of the hula dancers performing on stage. Eventually I joined him on the floor, where he was chatting it up with a pack of too-skinny, tween-looking girls in too-short miniskirts. Hello? You're on a date with me, remember?

He told me he just liked to talk to people.

WTF? Did he have ADHD or something?

The whole night gave me a bad vibe, so while I stayed with him in his hotel suite (I live in an old fourth floor walk-up apartment. Why not bask in soft sheets and panoramic views at a five-star hotel?), I decided to be careful and not have sex with him. I wanted to find out if he really liked me or not. That meant doing something I don't usually do.

I looked at his phone.

The next morning, while he was in the shower, he received a text. I picked up the phone. It was from a girl.

Okay, I couldn't really allow myself to be annoyed too much. He wasn't my boyfriend or anything. Then I opened his phone. There I saw texts from girls in every state in the USA! He even had a special system to classify them—their name with their state next to it. When I got to my name, it just said "Mary" with no New York.

Maybe someone else was "New York"? Or did the fact that he didn't have my last name down as the state I lived in mean that he had more respect for me than the others?

Whatever. At least the view of Central Park from the hotel suite was breathtaking.

By the time my "relationship" with Rico Suave was over, I had also returned to my previous job working with the over-eighty set, so he was my final work-related romance.

That is, until a really hot eighty-year-old makes his move.

Just kidding.

What did I learn from my on-the-job romances?

- Be spontaneous. Life is too short to hold back.

- Money is nice—if the guy has class. A cocky guy who shows off his money is a total turn-off.

- It's nice to be the bright spot in someone's day— even if that someone is an alcoholic octogenarian.

Five

Seeing the Sites

With work essentially off the table as a place to meet guys, I have, like so many millions of single women, turned to the Internet as a way to find suitable men. If you've ever taken part in the modern ritual of online dating, you already know: Internet dating can be bizarre. I know, dating in general tends to be bizarre—at least when I am involved. However, Internet dating comes with its own unique set of quirks. I don't think I'm exaggerating (at least not much) when I say that no woman has experienced more of those quirks than me.

For example, when you sign up for an online dating site, one of the many, many benefits is that you can check and see who has looked at your profile. What's a profile, you might ask if you're an online dating virgin? Here's my latest version on OKCupid:

Motto: Slightly imperfect—and stronger than yesterday
　　Classy, sassy, educated, funny, and worldly—just trying to get ahead in this concrete jungle!
　　I am: All heart (sometimes too much) and a big

personality. I have a zest for life and new experiences—especially travel.

I love: Running in Central Park, sipping martinis, lounging at home with good company, cooking, and discovering new neighborhoods.

I'm a mix of education and street smarts. I have conquered many obstacles in my life that have defined the strong, confident person I am today.

I'm really good at: Making people laugh, cooking, listening.

The first things people usually notice about me: My eyes.

Favorite books, movies, shows, music, and food: Mediterranean and Mexican food; Reese's Pieces Sundaes. I read magazines backwards. I can listen to anything—depends on my mood and what I want to accomplish.

The six things I could never do without: Music, my best friends (who are like family), heels, gloss, laughter, martinis with olives, running sneakers, and my passport. Yes, I know that's more than six but I'm a woman, so I get a pass on numbers 7 and 8.

A little more about me:

I like to travel and plan one big trip a year.

I enjoy meeting new and exciting people and picking their brains, learning something new, and carrying away a bit of insight that will stay with me forever.

I love anything that has to do with the ocean—I even like to fish!

I love Mediterranean food and bleu-cheese-stuffed olives.

I'm seeking a partner in crime to experience new and exciting things with me. Let's have fun!!

You must make me laugh—this is very important. I'm sure I can crack you up, and I expect the same.

Please resemble your profile pictures.

You should message me if: If you like my profile and are not going to jerk me around, let's meet for coffee OR crack a bottle of bubbly in Central Park.

I will not respond to a wink. I'm tired of being winked at. Please send an email. Winking is being lazy!

So, that's my profile.

Now, if you've already dipped a toe in the online dating waters, you might have experienced the strange phenomenon of guys checking out your profile but not sending a message, or even viewing your profile *multiple times* and still making no effort to actually communicate with you!

What's up with that? Do they just like looking at pictures and reading interesting facts about girls, like what kind of food they like and how important a sense of humor is in their world?

Of course, eventually, somebody (and probably several somebodies) will take the plunge and actually send you an email. Which doesn't mean you should get overly excited or anything, because eight times out of ten, that email will consist of less than four words.

Possibilities include:

"Hi, Hello."

"You are beautiful."

"You are sexy."

"What's up?"

And my personal favorite: The smiley face icon, which isn't a word at all!

They don't even leave their names. I don't get it. I feel like asking these guys, "Were your fingers not working that day and a smiley face was all you could possibly produce? Is there some new law I don't know about that forbids people from writing a complete sentence?"

I don't know why "potentials" bother to write at all when they can't even muster up the energy to give you their name. If a guy just emails "hello" or "you're hot," I'm not going to reply. Sure, we all know that dating is a game, but as long as I'm playing, I want to be a master.

Then there are the pictures. You can amass quite a photo collection through online dating websites. Many of those photos will bear absolutely no resemblance to the man they've been posted to represent. Not just in terms of physical features, but of personality.

Many, many, *many* of them.

How do I know all this? Because over the years I have become a seasoned veteran of the online dating game. I've learned that, while there are certain rules that apply across the board, each individual site has its own unique charms. And there are a LOT of these sites to choose from. In fact, I actually organize my online dates in my phone according to what website I met them on. My trick? I replace their last name with the site name. Some examples: Jim-Cupid, Bob-HOW (for How About We), Tony-Match, Joey-POF (Plenty of Fish).

Of course, just because there are a lot of sites out there doesn't mean they'll all be right for you. So to spare you the trouble of wasting time on the wrong site, I'm going to share the pros and cons (at least as my friends and I have experienced them) of the most popular dating sites.

Of course, I'm always open to learning more. So if you vigorously pursue this man safari and happen to bag a winner, I hope you'll share your success story so I can join up before all the good ones are gone.

One final note: The emails and stories that I've included here are NOT representative of all men on these sites (Just most of them!). Don't get me wrong. I have had my share of very lovely dates, but those would be too boring to write about. So I am simply sharing the highlights (or lowlights) of what I've experienced, so you'll know what to expect when the crazies come a-callin'.

Ready? The tour starts now!

First Stop – Match.com

We're starting our tour with Match.com for one big reason: size. Match, as we veterans call it, consistently ranks as one of the largest dating sites in the world, at least according to Hitwise and other statistic-gathering websites. What that means for you is more potential dates in your area just waiting to meet you.

Or someone.

Match.com also claims that over 250,000 people a year find a partner through its site. Which means that if you're going to try a dating site, Match is definitely worth looking into—especially if you're new to the online dating game.

Now, for my personal opinion:

Match is an okay site.

However, I've also discovered that many of the guys on Match also have profiles up on other dating sites. Plus, Match kind of makes me feel as though I'm sitting at a busy singles bar instead of at home on my couch. "Hit me again, Sam!"

I will now share some real-life encounters with emails from men who contacted me on Match.com.

Email: *I am a man. I have a functional brain, better than average cerebral functionality, and aptly dispense witticisms and humor at well-timed intervals. I desire you to speak with me. Please do comply, or I will malfunction, mechanically deconstruct, and turn into a potato. A messy, melty, cyber-potato-shell-of-a-human. And it will be your fault. By the way, I send this to everyone. I find it to be a techno-financially facilitated mechanism for pairing; I am a laser-beacon of romance!*

Also, I don't do work functions unless you have a fun job. Like if you're a clown, or a sniper, or for some reason a clown-sniper, which would make you hilariously dangerous and consequently, wildly attractive. Hit me up, shorty!

Okay, some of his lines were funny. But seriously, if you want a freak show, go to the circus. My response?

DELETE.

Email: *Hi, We are not what we each want in a match, but if you want to enjoy some great sex, let me know. I have a large penis.*

Chaz

FYI, Chaz's profile reads:

Video games are my main source of entertainment, but it is not required that my partner plays, just as long as she understands. It is better to know where your guy is at night when he is on the computer hanging out with his friends playing video games compared to other guys who may be with their friends at a bar doing something stupid. It also has the added bonus of being a very economical source of entertainment. I am looking for a woman who will be my best friend that I go and do things with, even if it is something I have never done before. Someone who will treat me the same way I treat them. That is also a sexual woman who has at least an average sex drive or higher. I am different than the norm. If you see that as positive then you are in for a treat.

Yikes. I felt sorry for the guy.

Of course, with the many, many men available on Match.com, you're bound to hook up with one eventually if you keep at it. Let's call mine Paulo. Here is our story.

Paulo

If you're one of those ladies who constantly bitches and moans about being a football widow, or about how your man ignores you, I have one word: Paulo. After connecting with this very hot Columbian on Match, we decided to meet for cocktails at The Living Room at the W Hotel.

Things looked promising at first, because Paulo looked extremely promising. His body was amazing, and so fine that he had submitted pictures of himself to *Playgirl*.

How do I know? Because he showed me!

He was also really, really smart. He was a successful entrepreneur who owned a coffee company. And did I mention foreign? Paulo seemed every inch the perfect match Match.com was promising.

But you know the saying: "If some is good, more is better." Let's call Paulo the exception that proves the rule. He was like a stray cat that you mistakenly feed once then winds up living on your doorstep or under your stairs. Forever after, even if you succeed in shooing him from your door (with a broom) and bolt it behind him, he'll pop right back up at your window, scratching and crying to get in.

In fact, while we saw each other for a few weeks, Paulo saw a lot more of me than I saw of him—because he more or less stalked me! He sent me messages telling me he was conveniently reading a book just outside places I had mentioned I would be. He even admitted to hanging out in a park, waiting to get a glimpse of me at an alumni networking event I said he couldn't come to.

On the plus side, that man just couldn't do enough for me. He was awesome enough to wake up at 4am with me to pick up my new doggie, Valentino, in New Jersey. He fixed everything in my apartment. He gave me hour-long massages. He even washed my feet—weird, but who doesn't enjoy a good foot rub! I have to admit: I liked the attention.

We became good friends, then lovers. Well, at least that's all I wanted it to be. The problem was, he always finagled his way into sleeping over, which led to my sneaking over to the couch in the middle of the night. The concept of personal space completely escaped him—he was always on top of me, always wanting to have sex, which, for some reason, I just wasn't into with him, even though he was amazing in bed.

I think maybe the thing that creeped me out about

Paulo was his double life. By day, he was a straight-arrow entrepreneur. By night, he was a swinger.

And not just any swinger, but a superstar on the NYC swingers' scene.

I don't know what damage was done to him as a child. Honestly, I'm no shrink and I really don't want to know, but his desperate need to be wanted and loved, at pretty much any price, speaks volumes. As does the fact that he was clearly not able to "fill up the deep hole" with any one woman.

So this particular Match.com match was not meant to be. However, I still take a turn on the dance floor with him once in a while—usually when I need something fixed in my apartment. And he's soooooo happy to do it. Why should I rob him of that joy and listen to a leaky faucet all night at the same time?

As I see it, it's a win-win.

Second Stop – eHarmony.com

Maybe you've seen the commercials for eHarmony. com, the ones where the kindly looking old guy who invented the site pops up in the middle of happy young couples' dates, proposals, and honeymoons. And he has a right to be proud. eHarmony is based on science—it uses a compatibility matching system that takes 29 different personality variables and uses them to figure out who you're most likely to have a good relationship with.

eHarmony is very strict about its magical dating formula. The site only allows users to contact people "the system" has decided is a good match for them. But that takes time. Sometimes it can take weeks or even months for the site to find enough "dates" to justify the cost of membership, which is pretty steep, compared to the other sites out there.

If you want to see how eHarmony's scientific magic works for you, here's a tip: If you hold out for a little while, you'll probably receive a whole bunch of emails from eHarmony down the line offering better prices—usually at the same time the site has found more potential matches for you to choose from.

I was only on eHarmony for three months before deleting my account. I hooked up with a guy I liked so much that I quit. But more on that later. It offers a whole buffet of unique services the other sites don't have, like confidential phone chat. Plus, the site boasts more users in Canada than any other dating site in the world!

Maybe I should consider a move up North.

Check out these genuine, eHarmony sanctioned dates, and you be the judge.

Baldy

One common complaint about dating websites is the great-looking (or at least acceptable-looking) photos posted on the site, which lead you to decide you want to meet said person. Then, when you show up at the bar or coffeehouse where you're supposed to have that first face-to-face, you walk right by the person you're supposed to be meeting because *they look nothing like their photo.* Some of them even post photos that are clearly ten years old. Like Baldy. I swear he had a full head of hair in his profile pictures. He could have been a hair model for all I knew, but that was clearly before our real-life encounter.

I don't mind dating bald guys as long as they're honest. At least post a picture from the current year. Anything else is false advertising.

I don't remember much about Baldy. I don't know what it was about him that the magical eHarmony compatibility matching gods determined was so very, very right for me. The main thing I remember was the giant bald spot on the top of his head (which is, of course, how he got his nickname). One that his photo conveniently neglected to show.

In fact, he looked nothing at all like his picture.

We went to a hookah bar in the East Village, where I soon discovered that not only was my date secretly bald; he was also a very finicky eater. That isn't a big deal, except that he wasn't exactly in shape. I couldn't quite figure out the purpose of all of his many food restrictions.

Physically, we were so mismatched I felt like people were staring at us. However, lest you think I'm totally shallow, I also remember that he was an absolutely horrible kisser.

The perfect ending to a perfect evening. Not.

Alejandro

Fortunately, Baldy wasn't the only man the eHarmony compatibility gods matched me up with. They also found the guy I call Alejandro, after the Lady Gaga song of the same name. If you've heard the song, you might suspect this is another rather bittersweet tale.

It is. But I promise I'll spare you the drunken, sobbing love poems I wrote to him after it all came to a tragic end.

Ohhhhh, Alejandro. The compatibility meter got it right that time—he was the one guy I fell for head over heels after my divorce. In fact, I think maybe, possibly, I was even in love with him. It was as though he put a spell on me: I was so incredibly emotionally and physically attracted to him, I couldn't keep my mind (or my hands) off the guy. I got butterflies in my stomach every time I saw him, even after a few months.

If I had a checklist, Alejandro was the one guy who ticked all the boxes. Of course, he was exotic—Argentinean this time. I can't seem to get enough of those Latin lovers. He was an ambitious entrepreneur who owned a bunch of clothing boutiques. He was smart, funny, and charming.

Oh yeah, and he had a motorcycle.

My first-ever motorcycle ride was on the back of Alejandro's bike, my arms wrapped around his waist. He literally swept me off my feet—I'll never forget the exhilarating sense of freedom as we flew down the Brooklyn Queens Expressway… Thinking I was going to die.

But I didn't.

Then there was the time he decided to book a romantic weekend away in the Poconos. If you're not from the East Coast, you might not be aware of Pennsylvania's cheesy honeymoon haven—a mountain town filled with little cabin motels and inns that seem to be designed for the sole purpose of hosting creative, crazy sexual encounters.

Before we even reached our destination, I guessed that our room was going to have a floor-to-ceiling glass bathtub shaped like a champagne glass and a heart-shaped bed (I'd seen enough corny Poconos commercials in the 1980s to have some idea of what to expect).

And I was right!

Our cabin had it all: the red velvet interior, the heart-shaped bed (plus a heart-shaped pool!), and of course, the obligatory, sky-high champagne glass tub. When the room wasn't booked, it was probably used as a set for porn videos.

We certainly found the space…inspiring.

After a few hours of indoor fun, we decided it was time to eat. Unfortunately, we showed up two hours after dinner service closed. The helpful kitchen lady threw some slimy green leftovers that resembled something I might step over on a New York street onto a plate.

Oh well. It wasn't really about the food anyway.

The time Alejandro and I spent together was a blast. It seemed like eHarmony definitely earned their pricey membership fee, which was why I happily left the site as a satisfied customer.

As we crept closer to that crucial three-month mark, though, things started getting weird. Then, like all good things, it came to an end.

It wasn't ugly or dramatic. We still talk occasionally. In fact, he recently shoved his tongue down my throat, which, I have to admit, helped with the healing process. Although it took a LOT of drunken sob poems to get there.

He even talks about the possibility of giving it another shot. I still get those butterflies every time I hear his voice, so you never know.

In the end, I learned a lot from dating Alejandro. I learned a lot about myself, and not only what I want in a guy (or what eHarmony's magic compatibility survey thinks I want in a guy), but about life in general.

I also learned that I am a really, really crappy poet.

Third Stop – OkCupid

OkCupid is not your mother's dating website. First of all, it's free! Second, it combines social networking (a la Facebook), compatibility testing (a la eHarmony) and the basic stuff you usually find with online dating (a la Match). Third, it actually allows you, the member, to create your own questions for your potential matches instead of restricting you to a predetermined list like eHarmony or Match. Plus, you're allowed to contact anyone on the system—even if the system thinks that person will be a terrible match for you. In fact, it categorizes your potential dates as an Enemy, Friend, or Match—so you can proceed at your own risk!

I did proceed, and the result is these real-life (I swear!) examples of the gems I've encountered on OkCupid.

Buffoon – AKA NYC Fitness Guy

I learned a lot about Buffoon—enough to give him that nickname—without ever meeting him. He kept sending me pictures of himself working out, and even thought to send a video of him running on the treadmill at the gym.

I assume he figured I'd catch a glimpse of his rock-hard bod and beg for an in-person meet up. Instead, my reaction was more along the lines of, "Why-oh-why? Will I EVER meet a normal guy in this city?" I felt sorry for the poor gym worker who was forced to record the sweaty beast in action. I asked for a picture, not a video of his candy (yet very nice), wildebeest ass huffing and puffing.

The guy was actually kind of cute, but the video, plus the twenty pictures of him working out, were anything but.

Then there was the fact that he sent *the exact same*

photos to a coworker of mine who had been chatting with him on another dating service.

NEXT!

I still have that video and share it with my friends for a good laugh—and to remind them to assess the prospects before agreeing to a date. More on that in Chapter 13.

Email: [Brachiosaurus77]

Yes. This guy actually named himself after a dinosaur. Kind of sweet…if you're eight years old. If the name wasn't enough to turn me off, his emails were.

Hey. Look. I'll admit it. I got a bit excited because it looks like you have some kind of properly balanced feminine energy going on there. I mean, don't get me wrong – it's not like I am some sort of hobbit out on a quest to find the ONE girliest girl to rule them all. I would say I'm more like Goldilocks in the story with the three bears, stealing porridge from these terribly vicious animals in a pompous and high-maintenance manner; complaining that NOTHING is acceptable to me except the one that is JUST right. Not extravagantly girly and not too tomboyish. I guess what I'm trying to say is that I am essentially a small girl with blonde hair that plunders vile, porridge-eating bears.

Yikes! Is that a dream lover or what? Unfortunately, Goldilocks was only just getting started.

Anyway, where are my manners?

Wow. All that and manners, too?

My name's Nelson and if smart, funny, stylish, cute, and overall just frankly awesome guys are your thing, then don't send me a message. Oh wait, I messed up. I mean DO send me a message. I get confused sometimes :)

Despite all his hard work, I did not respond.

But after a few weeks, just like Freddy, he was baaaaaack. No doubt after waking from a long nap in Baby Bear's bed, 'cause it was <u>just right</u>!

Hey,

So I was checking my account today in utter disbelief that I didn't hear back from you yet, and then I just realized what must have happened to you. You must have been burglarized, and the only thing that horrible and wretched thief had to have stolen was your keyboard. I feel bad now you poor, poor soul... you must have been so traumatized just sitting there staring at my profile on the screen, clicking away futilely and slamming your mouse down in frustration multiple times while cursing the heavens that this had to happen to you today and that there's no way for you respond to me. Like I said... luckily for you, I'm an exceptionally perceptive guy. I mean how many other guys would know that is EXACTLY what happened to you with the limited information you gave me :). And since I'm also in the business of solving problems, here's some solutions to help you get in contact with me: 1.Get some matches, grab three garbage cans, and arrange them in a triangle formation to set them all on fire simultaneously. This will create an accurate smoke triangulation signal so I can come over and find you. I'm like a modern-day knight in shining armor. 2. Use your trusty phone to text me at [646-xxx-xxxx] so we can continue the conversation.

I chose option #3: DELETE!

Not to completely slam OkCupid—my former roommate did find love on the site and she's now living with the guy. So, you never know.

Fourth Stop – Plenty of Fish

Known simply as POF to its forum users, Plenty of Fish is considered the first successful free dating site model on the Internet. It's still owned and operated by the same person, Markus Frind, even though his user base outnumbers most of the pay-per-use websites in North America. The sheer number of people all over the world using this feature-rich site (including heavily-trafficked forums, compatibility questionnaires, and the super-popular Who's Seen Me button) is astronomical, making this site incredibly powerful in its ability to connect people around the globe looking for friendship, love, and anything in between.

That said, it hasn't exactly hooked me up with any winners. Maybe that saying, "You get what you pay for" does hold true.

Perhaps a friend of mine put it best when she recently posted on Facebook:

I need to make a POF profile again. Life's boring without strange men sending me dick pics, offers for threesomes, and asking how much money would it take for me to piss on them.

As for me, well, I did meet one winner.

Questionable Attire

After hooking up via POF, I had a few dates with a correctional officer. I believe that is the polite term for prison guard. Anyway, we made it all the way to the point when we were ready to seal the deal. And we did.

I woke up the next morning and was aghast to see what was covering the ass lying next to me. The man I just spent the night with had dressed up for our big evening together by putting on a pair of Homer Simpson boxer shorts.

D'oh!

Oh—he was also thirty-five years old.

Fifth Stop – Skout

Now, for those of you who are sticklers for accuracy, Skout is not technically an online dating website. It's a smartphone app designed to help you hook up with new "friends" based on your location. Seeing as I live in a neighborhood full of gay guys, Skout seemed like an ideal way to cut through the perfectly groomed clutter and find a man interested in XX chromosomes.

The fine folks at Skout make safety a priority—so they separate the sites into two communities: one for grown-ups, one for teenagers. The latter is perhaps where the most memorable guy I Skout-ed actually belonged.

Werewolf

Werewolf claimed to be a former rock star. At least he was a former rock *performer*—his major claim to fame was that his band once opened for Metallica back in the '90s. By the time I met him, his guitar-playing, wannabe-rock-god days were behind him and he'd become something of a Renaissance man—and had racked up an unusually large array of pursuits and specialties. He was a magician, a ghost buster (seriously!), a Reiki healer, and a pilot who simultaneously grew organic facial products from some Amazon mud he collected.

He was also a former ventriloquist. I learned this fact the hard way, when I entered his dimly lit apartment for the very first time. Lined up against the living room wall was a veritable parade of Chucky-like dolls (you know, the doll with the knife from the movie "Child's Play") looking like they could go full-Chucky on me, come to life, and kill me at any second.

The warning signs kept coming. A dinner date with Werewolf revealed he was manorexic—when I helped myself to a piece of bread from the basket on the table, he glared at me like I'd just taken a big bite of a stick of butter. He thought carbs were some kind of devil's snack food and avoided them at all costs.

Like any physical fitness freak, Werewolf also spent between three and four hours a day at the gym, every day, followed by a rip-roaring session of Bikram hot yoga.

Oh yeah, he was fit—physically at least.

By now you know I'm a sucker for a guy who keeps in shape (as long as I don't have to see a video of him running on a treadmill), but Werewolf was more than that. He was some kind of crazy genius (as evidenced by his amazingly diverse range of careers) and had the whole "bad boy" thing going on, which I loved—right down to the piercing of his penis.

Unfortunately, our dates weren't quite as exciting as he was. We spent most of our time hanging around his apartment, where I watched him play his guitar; watched videos from his big-haired, rock star "heyday"; and worried about one of those Chucky dolls taking me out when I wasn't looking.

We had been out about six times (practically going steady for me!) when Halloween rolled around, so I invited him to my apartment for a party, after which the whole group was going to go out on the town—in costume, of course.

In case you're wondering, this is the part of the story where Werewolf got his name.

One of his *other* many careers (I can't possibly remember them all!) was as a theatrical make-up artist. Halloween was truly his holiday to howl. He arrived at my apartment in the most convincing werewolf costume I've ever seen.

That's when the fun started.

One of my guests was a friend named Jennifer—who now happens to be a former friend. She was dressed as an angel, but things went to hell when she locked eyes with the sexy monster I had been dating.

The three of us ended up sharing a cab to the after party, but five blocks before our destination, Werewolf jumped out of the cab, claiming he had to piss so badly he couldn't hold it another second.

I knew better. He didn't need to pee—he just didn't want to pay.

During our entire night on the town, my date, who had at least $100 worth of makeup on his face, bought me one drink, and I pretty much had to squeeze that out of him. Then, true to his magician roots, he completely disappeared. Turns out, he and my angel friend slipped out together, sharing a cab back home to our neighborhood.

I wonder who paid.

I also met a millionaire on Skout who conveniently forgot to tell me he was married! He told me about an hour into our date. WTF?

Sixth Stop – Tinder

Like Skout, Tinder is designed for smartphones, but unlike Skout, it's a lot more "grown up" and much more popular with people my age. Rules are swipe right if you're interested in someone or swipe left if you're not. I downloaded the Tinder app for fun (and research!) on a recent vacation to Australia and continue to receive matches from guys in Australia and New Zealand. Too bad I live in the USA; although, there is one guy who wants me to get him a green card.

I did manage to line up a handful of American Tinder dates and this one will likely be my last. Warning: Be careful what you wish for when you swipe right because your date may end up looking like THIS Tinder Winner.

Tinder Ezra

Ezra was thirty-six, Jewish, and the head of some mobile app company.

He was also a complete tool.

I met him at a local bar in my 'hood at what he called the "Tinder table." He had a very dry sense of humor. Unfortunately, I did not find anything he said remotely humorous. He even made the poor waitress feel uncomfortable! He also kept checking his phone for work messages, which is one of my biggest pet peeves.

Maybe he was just a little nervous, because in the two hours we spent at the bar, he chugged down about six drinks. During that time I learned that he is willing to marry a non-Jewish girl and give her a Christmas tree, but he must raise his children Jewish. Oh, and that he's been circumcised.

Good to know.

I also got the impression he felt I was used goods or something because I'm divorced. When I told him my ex was Turkish, his biggest concern was his idea that Turkish men are "all hairy."

As the night progressed, things got stranger. He told me the muddled cherry in my drink looked like a vagina. Ummm…okay. Then he compared his penis to a cherry stem. I guess he had some weird sexual obsession with cherries. I'm not planning a second date to find out why.

Seventh Stop – JDate

Of course, if you really want to meet a Jewish guy, there's a dating site just for you. Even more good news—you don't have to be Jewish to join JDate!

My friend signed me up for JDate, even though I am not Jewish myself. She simply clicked "willing to convert" under the drop-down menu where you are asked the age-old question, "What kind of Jew are you?"

I'm not actually willing to convert to anything, but I was definitely curious to see what types of guys were available to choose from among the Chosen People. Turns out a lot of them are 5'10 and under, have a PhD, and/or are doctors or lawyers.

I wasn't intrigued enough to fork out money for the membership fee, so I can't tell you much more about the site. I can report that guys were emailing me left and right and I didn't even put any pictures up! As a non-paying browser, I never found out what any of those emails said, but for all you *shiksas* looking for a guy with a promising career (just not in the NBA), JDate could be your Promised Land.

Eighth Stop – How About We

What if a dating website skipped all the question-naires and compatibility quizzes and got right down to the nitty-gritty: the date? That's the beauty of How About We, my current favorite among all the dating websites available.

As we're now on number eight, you know I've been to just about all of them!

How About We flips the script on traditional online dating—because the date itself is already planned, there is no need for endless back-and-forth messaging (a blessing). The way it works is you actually propose a date online—something like "How About We…go to a Knicks game?" Or "How About We…check out that new Korean restaurant?"

That makes How About We the only dating site that really helps the user get offline and on real dates with real people! As one user put it, "The date proposal is the ultimate digital first impression."

The second impression, unfortunately, is up to the user.

Crazy Eyes

Crazy Eyes was the second guy I met on How About We, but definitely first when it comes to memorable experiences.

On our first date ("How About We…go hear some live jazz?"), I just couldn't shake the feeling that something was a little off. For starters, there were the eyes that inspired his nickname. I tried to ignore the fact that they looked a bit like the eyes of a mental patient, or worse.

I also remember checking my phone and hearing him comment about seeing an email from a dating site in my inbox. He was looking over my shoulder! Hello, it's our first date—why are you creeping up behind me?!

I agreed to a second date, because I like to give people the benefit of the doubt.

This, in retrospect, was not a good idea.

He had a big evening planned. It started with dinner at a Russian restaurant. I couldn't help noticing how deeply and intensely he stared at me when he spoke, and that he stared at the waiter the same way. It was as though he was trying to convey a piece of life-or-death information. Not that he would like to start with the cold beet borscht.

Seriously, this man did not blink. I almost had to stop myself from laughing because I caught myself wondering if his eyes hurt from the effort of staying wide open at all times.

During dinner, I learned that he had moved more than half a dozen times—all around the country—after graduating college. That added to my general sense that this guy was just a bit unstable.

After dinner, we went to see a play called "Avenue Q," which was a huge hit at the time. We came in thirty minutes late, but I forgave him since we had front row seats. I guess he was a huge fan, because he had already seen the play twice before he took me. My mind started racing again. Why would anyone want to see the same play three times? Is this where he brings all his dates?

It turned out the play was really funny. I laughed aloud quite a few times. Every time I laughed, I felt my date's giant dark eyes burning a hole through the left side of my face. I actually *felt* him staring. It was that intense.

So, I'd turn to look at him, and he'd comment. He said things like, "It really wasn't that funny," or, "Why are you laughing?" Yikes. It wasn't *Hamlet* or anything. It was a funny play! I was having fun, so I ignored his weirdness.

After the play, he walked me home, because I live on the same block as the theater. That, my friends, is when I took my own little detour into Crazy Town. I invited him up to my apartment for a drink. That may be the dumbest thing I have ever done in my entire life.

As expected, the conversation got weird fast. I told him my dad had passed away. He told me his dad—or maybe his mom, I don't remember—had passed away, too. What were the chances of his parent conveniently dying a mere five weeks after mine? The mind boggles. As our conversion continued, he grew increasingly agitated for no reason, until he started flipping out on me. In my apartment! On our second date! He started yelling things such as, "it's always about you" and "your feelings" and "what about me?"

Yikes!

Needless to say, I was scared out of my mind. I knew I had to think of something to get this psychopath out of my apartment before he chopped me up into itty-bitty pieces and left me in a garbage bag on the sidewalk.

So I very, very calmly said, "You need to put your shoes on and go home." He did, which no doubt is why I'm still here, writing this today.

He texted me when he got home, apologizing profusely for his actions and saying he understood why I might have been scared.

Might have been scared? I was *this close* to calling 9-1-1.

I ignored the message. Two days later, he texted me another apology. It included some very wise advice—something along the lines of, "You should follow your instinct, it is usually right."

So, I trusted mine, and never, ever communicated with him again.

Ninth Stop – Sugar Time!

Okay, I fudged this one a little. Our ninth and final stop is not a dating site. It's a whole category of dating sites geared toward one big idea: that what women are really looking for in a man is a big, huge, massive pile of cash.

I've never been a fan of these sites. Any guy who cares so much about showing off his bankroll that he'd sign up for a dating site that's basically designed to attract gold diggers (or can't get a woman any other way) is probably not going to be the man of my dreams.

However, ever since her experience with my ex's gun-wielding rug haggler back in Turkey, my friend Zoe developed a taste for the finer things and decided to seek greener (as in money) dating pastures when we got back to New York. Seekingarrangement.com and Sugardaddyforme.com became her go-to sites for hooking up with rich, successful men who were in the market for young women who didn't mind being "bought."

While I was spending my evenings with corrections officers and wannabe ventriloquists, my girl was busy traveling the world with her online hookups and had amassed a wardrobe to rival Victoria Beckham's.

I started thinking, why not? I could never bring myself to sign up for Seeking Arrangement—money might be nice, but love is still essential. But maybe the guys on these sites were a little more mature, a little more together. Maybe these sites would finally separate the men from the boys. Maybe I would finally be able to meet a real man and cancel that Match.com subscription.

Seeking Millionaire

I know, I know, the name sounds a little creepy, but this site advertises itself as a dating website matching rich, successful, upscale, established, or millionaire singles with the gorgeous, attractive, cute, and beautiful. I'd at least like to consider myself cute! According to the site, its members include executives, celebrities, doctors, lawyers, professional athletes, investors, entrepreneurs, CEOs—you name it. As I filled out my profile, I actually felt excited.

Unfortunately, the millionaire I ended up with was not exactly the millionaire I was seeking.

Asian Spiderman

Initially, my millionaire did have some attributes I found semi-appealing. He was Asian (not my usual flavor of foreign, but still foreign), in his forties (the younger end of the millionaire dating pool), and he wasn't bad looking, especially in the dimly lit lounges that millionaires apparently like to frequent.

We made it to the crucial third date, so we of course found ourselves headed to his apartment—a place in Chelsea he shared with a fellow countryman. That's when the games began.

It appeared my millionaire made at least some of his money as a member of Cirque du Soleil.

I've never experienced anything like it. The guy was an amazing acrobat. He could climb until he was literally hanging from the ceiling—hence the nickname Asian Spiderman. Unfortunately, what hung down was teeny-weeny, if you get my drift.

But hey, I'm not going to break it off with a potentially nice guy, let alone a potentially nice millionaire, just because of his endowment (or lack thereof). So the next week, we were off to Atlantic City, along with a girlfriend of mine he generously let me bring along.

At least, that's what I thought. After a night on the town, I drowsily emerged from my alcohol-induced slumber only to find Asian Spiderman hooking up with my friend—while she was asleep!

Of course, that was the last time I saw the little spider, but he did send flowers the next week and still texts me from time to time.

But here's the best part: I later found out he was MARRIED!

DELETE!

MillionaireMatch.com

Who wants to be matched with a millionaire? I did, until I paid a visit to this site and met this very confused member.

Mistaken Identity

It all seemed very straightforward: The matchmakers at millionairematch.com had matched me with a loaded dentist in his forties. I was excited—I figured that if he was single and in his forties, he'd most likely already been screwed up by a former relationship and was ready to settle down with the "the one." He was interested in me, or so I thought.

We exchanged pictures—no problems there. We spoke on the phone a few times. Again, no warning signs. We finally agreed to meet at Blue Water Grill, a seafood restaurant in Union Square. We met out front and were immediately seated at a wonderful table.

Here's where things started to get really—how should I put this—otherworldly.

As we sat down together at this wonderful table in this lovely restaurant, the look on MI's face was anything but wonderful and lovely. It was more like perplexed. What could possibly be the problem? We had exchanged pictures. We had spoken on the phone. When he opened his mouth to explain his distress, what came out was definitely one for the books:

"You're not the girl I was supposed to meet!"

WTF?

He looked just like his picture, as did I. We both arrived at the pre-designated time and place. What could possibly be the problem? My personal, self-preserving assumption is that I looked so good that night it simply freaked him out.

As we sat there in utter disbelief (me, especially), the poor waiter made three separate attempts to take our order, while we bantered back and forth about his true identity. I still have no idea exactly what happened or how, but we ultimately agreed that the best solution was for each of us to run as far away from the other as fast as our little legs could carry us.

It was raining and windy that night, and by the time I stormed into the subway, my umbrella had blown inside out. I called a friend to relay my completely unbelievable tale of woe just as an extremely nice gentleman walked over to me and asked what was wrong.

I gave him a thirty-second synopsis, and he invited me out to dinner then and there. And you know what? We had the BEST time! A truly wonderful evening and a true New York moment.

Who says chivalry is dead?

I never did hear from the dentist again, but I assume he spends his days inhaling nitric oxide and mixing up his poor patients. I can hear them now: "But doctor, I just came in for a cleaning and you extracted my four front teeth!"

VIP Life

VIP Life isn't technically a dating site. It's a good old-fashioned matchmaking service designed for very determined "shoppers" with a singular goal in mind: to bag the really big game. Or, according to the VIP Life website, "it attracts the most beautiful and sophisticated women interested in having a long-term relationship with dynamic and attractive men who have proven their success within the business community, and want to meet women of exceptional beauty, grace, and substantive intellect. Membership is complimentary to qualified women so there is no access barrier to women of quality and substance."

According to its founder, president, and all-time big-game hunter, Lisa Clampitt, her stable of super-successful guys are all superstars in their own right, having reached the top in whatever they do. Beyond that, however, they're just like you and me—looking for that special someone with whom to share life's pleasures. An article in *Forbes* states that the club pulls in up to $20,000 a year per client helping people who have been looking for love in all the wrong places. That is a lot of money for the privilege of looking! But hey, if you've got the green, then why not?

I, on the other hand, did not have the green. Luckily, ladies are accepted into the club for free, provided they "qualify."

Well, I'm always up for a challenge. So I sent in my pictures through the website and was thrilled to learn I passed the initial test. I was called into an office in Union Square for a personal interview. There, I was disheartened to find myself winding my way through piles and piles of women's profiles and photos stretching from floor to ceiling.

Those didn't look like very good odds to me. I guess that's what the men get for their $20K.

However, I received the ultimate seal of approval when I was accepted by VIP Life and added to the giant pile 'o ladies. Five months later, I got a call to meet a prospective date, but didn't feel that spark when we met. I just didn't find him both emotionally stimulating and physically attractive enough to go through with a second date. I didn't feel the chemistry I had so hoped for with VIP Life.

Maybe it worked for Anna Nicole Smith, but a big bankroll just isn't enough to win my heart. Eventually, I learned through my tour of millionaire dating sites and services that money can't buy me love. Plus, I don't want to be pushing my husband around in a wheelchair. I get enough of that at work!

With that, we conclude our whirlwind tour of the online dating world. Have you learned a lot? Because God knows, I have!

Just to be sure, let's recap...

- If you get a weird feeling in your belly that something just ain't right on a first date, it probably isn't.

- Your time is precious. Follow your instincts and it won't steer you wrong. Plus, you will save on calories and beauty sleep for your next first date with another guy— who could be a real keeper!

- Never trust a guy who doesn't blink.

- Money can't buy you love and happiness. This is the twenty-first century—we women should be able to comfortably support ourselves. Any self-respecting gentleman will be attracted to a woman who has it going on in both her career and personal life.

- Some men are just weird. And not in a fun way.

Six

Foreign Intrigue

By now, you're already well versed in my love of foreign men. But the few I've talked about so far—my ex-husband, Alejandro, and the other various tall, dark, and handsome would-be partners who have graced these pages—represent a mere fraction of the foreign-born who have stamped my dating passport. There are more. So many more. And, lucky you! You get to meet a couple of them right here.

Germ Sperm

What could be classier than a guy nicknamed "Germ Sperm"?

A guy who actually nicknames *himself* "Germ Sperm"!

Honestly, it's not as bad as it sounds. First of all, he called himself Germ Sperm because he's German. Not exactly an excuse, but at least it's an explanation that doesn't involve an STD, right? Plus, he was incredibly, totally, severely hot. He was 6'5", with the kind of body you'd expect from a one-time pro rugby player—which he was back in his native land.

He also had an awesome personality (as evidenced by his self-nicknaming sense of humor), a huge you-know-what, and, my personal favorite trait in a potential mate, he was still learning English! (Does it say something about me that I prefer guys who can't actually communicate with me in words? Oh well, I guess that's one for my therapist.)

When I was introduced to the Germ Sperm through a friend, I definitely thought I hit the jackpot. He worked for an international real estate company that exported him into my life via a U.S. work visa. There was just one small problem. The company was based just outside of Holmes County, Ohio, which is right up there with Pennsylvania for boasting one of the largest Amish communities in the country.

This meant my new foreign obsession actually did live in another country—the Midwest.

Once a month, he would hop on a plane and leave the cow pastures and Amish people for the bright lights of NYC, and we would hang out and have an insanely wild time together.

This went on (well, off and on) for three years. I really liked Germ Sperm (as ridiculous as it feels to write those words). I had a blast when I was with him, and when we were apart, we would spend countless hours on the phone just being silly. It never turned into anything too serious, though, because there was no way on earth I could ever, ever move to Ohio.

I need restaurants. Stores. Civilization.

Still, I felt like I could tell him anything and I thought he could tell me anything—including who we were dating. I guess I secretly hoped we would maybe end up together one day. I felt like the connection we had was so strong that we were meant to be.

Once again (this is getting to be a habit with me), I was wrong.

I knew he had been dating some chick in Atlanta, but when I arrived home from a vacation in Spain (more on my foreign travels later), his Facebook status suddenly said, "Married"!

Married?

WTF?!

He married Atlanta!

Exactly when did that fall through the cracks? At this point, I still don't know. Maybe he was afraid it would upset me. Maybe it did—a little—but even though I wish them nothing but happiness, my instinct tells me they'll probably end up divorced in a few years.

In the meantime, at least Germ Sperm has his green card. If he ever gets out of Ohio (and, of course, his marriage), I hope he gives me a call.

Kartrashian Countryman

Just like that famous-for-being-famous family, this particular foreign import came to me from the faraway land of Armenia. I met him at the rooftop bar at the Gansevoort Hotel. It was dark. I now use that as an excuse for the fact that I actually went home with this slimeball.

Yes, this is one of *those* dates.

The KC, who I also sometimes call Creeper, seemed like he was on the up-and-up. He told me he worked for the U.N. and was in town on government business—something

I have since learned is a very popular line amongst foreign guys looking to score. We shared a couple of cocktails and the usual idle chatter, and he seemed nice enough that when he invited me back to his place, like the fool I too often am, I accepted.

The first red flag came when we were in the cab, heading down Orchard Street to his apartment. Except, he couldn't remember what the number of his apartment was. I thought that was a little strange, but we had been drinking, and he was from Armenia, so maybe he wasn't home much? Anyway, eventually he remembered which apartment was "his."

But when we got to the door, someone else was behind it.

KC explained that this was a guy who worked for him putting gas in his car. "Wow," I wondered, "how much do you pay a guy for that?" I never found out, because the guy promptly left. I guess to go pump some gas.

I stayed the night, although I did not sleep with KC in the biblical sense. When I woke up in the morning, my new Armenian friend was nowhere in sight, but I was not without male company.

Yes, the gas-pumping guy had returned! Here's the very best part. When I queried him as to where KC might be found, he said he was PUTTING GAS IN THE CAR!

Oops.

The maybe-not-a-gas-pumping-guy must have instantly realized his mistake, because he blew that Popsicle stand in what felt like seconds. Me? I wanted out of there, too, but not until I did a little CSI New York-style investigating. I wanted to know exactly who this Casanova was.

Sadly, years on the dating scene have turned me into a very seasoned sleuth.

I threw my clothes on and scanned the apartment for any identifying material. I spotted a backpack on the floor, opened it up, and, voila: Inside was a checkbook with KC's name on top and what I imagine was his wife's name right under it, unless he had a joint checking account with his sister or his mother. It also indicated that he was some kind of military person who apparently lived in Pensacola.

Clearly, this was not a love connection. I wanted a memento, so I ripped out a check that I would later use to google KC for more info. I also contemplated sending the check to his wife, but ultimately decided I'd done enough damage.

What kind of damage, you might ask?

I wanted to leave KC something to remember *me* by, so I turned on every faucet in the place full blast and stuffed the drains with towels. Then I ran out of the building, hailed a cab, and rode home with the satisfied smile of a woman who had just flooded out a jumbo sewer rat.

What have I learned from the foreign guys I've dated?

- Think twice about leaving the club with a guy who says he "works for the U.N."

- Jump out of the cab at the next red light if your date can't remember his apartment number. Side note: If he can't remember his apartment number, he probably will also not remember to send you a "good morning beautiful" text.

- Don't suppress your true feelings for a male friend because you're afraid of scaring him away. You only live once, and you'll never know how "good" a friend he can be until you share your secret! Worst case scenario: He'll be flattered. Best case: You can tell your kids the story of how you married your best friend.

Seven
On the Road

Ever since that semester I spent in England when I was twenty, I've lived to travel. That trip was my first time out of the country—before then, I had only been to Florida, which is kind of like the very, very south end of New York. In other words, Florida is about as far from exotic as a trip to Hoboken.

I made the most of my first experience outside the continental U.S. of A. I didn't just stick around England. I visited Scotland, and crossed over to mainland Europe to travel all over Italy, spend a weekend in Paris, journey to Austria, and even hop over to Germany for a day for Oktoberfest. I think the highlight was my trip to the island of Capri, where I fell in love with anything and everything Mediterranean.

By the time I got back home to Long Island, I was a totally different person. The travel bug had bitten me hard. I don't think I'll ever recover from the effects.

Before I even made it to Turkey with Burak, I had learned that there's an amazing world out there and so much to see, and I want to see as much of it as I possibly can. I need to feel like I'm a part of something greater and bigger than just going to work and serial dating, so I try to plan one big trip a year, and that trip is never to a place I've been before (no matter how much I love it). After all, I'm a girl on a budget.

As a result, my passport has a whole lot of stamps in it, including:

- England

- Scotland

- France

- Austria

- Germany

- Italy

- Turkey

- Costa Rica

- Spain

- Bermuda

- The Bahamas

- South Africa

- St. Kitts

- Australia

- Fiji

- Greece

- Honduras

Of course, dining on yummy worldly cuisine and seeing the sights is only part of what I experience when I travel. My favorite activity is to soak up the local culture. Sometimes that includes a little romance. After all, meeting guys while traveling combines two of my greatest passions: exotic men and exotic places!

Costa Rican Gilberto

For many years, my best girl Zoe was my traveling companion of choice. There was a point when I decided to start going solo because her crazy sexual energy tends to eclipse everything else within a five-mile radius, including me. She was with me on this particular trip to Costa Rica, however, and as usual, in a matter of what seemed like seconds, Zoe had hooked up with the pick of the local litter: The hot hotel lifeguard/surf instructor, whom we nick-named Puss in Boots.

So off went Zoe to make sweet jungle love in a tree with her newfound Latin stud, leaving me by my lonesome. I headed down to the beach, where I met Gilberto, a local tour guide. We chatted for about an hour, and when Zoe and her man-of-the-moment finally climbed down from the tree, the four of us decided to have dinner together.

Gilberto and I became a twosome, too. My second night out with Gilberto, we left Zoe and Puss behind for what Gilberto billed as a drive "into the wilderness." I figured that because he was a tour guide he knew what he was doing, so we drove and drove, and then he pulled his car onto a deserted road off the beaten path by the beach.

We got out of the car and made out under the pale moonlight. What could be more romantic?

Turns out, just about anything. Almost the minute our lips touched, my skin began to itch and burn like crazy. I was covered with ants, and they found me even tastier than Gilberto did!

At least I hope they were ants, and not some rare poisonous tropical insects that will nest in my bloodstream for the next twenty years and manifest in some rare form of malaria.

Gilberto tried to count just how many ant bites I had sustained, but there were so many, he lost track. However, an exotic insect attack was only the beginning of our tropical adventure. As I stood there scratching furiously, we suddenly heard what sounded like a couple of guys walking on the empty beach.

Gilberto immediately clamped his hand over my mouth (my hands were otherwise engaged with the scratching) and whispered to be quiet, as men appearing in the dark on deserted stretches of Costa Rican beach usually come with weapons.

I thought I was going to die. Then again, considering the agony I was experiencing, it might have been a mercy kill.

But there was no beachside shakedown, and no kidnapping for ransom. Gilberto got me back to the hotel safe and sound, albeit a little itchy. Zoe and I succeeded in counting the bites. It turned out there were sixty-four of them. After a good night's sleep, or as good a night's sleep as a person can have while covered with fresh ant bites (thank God for calamine lotion!), I was ready for another round of fun and frolic with my new friend the next night.

This time, I met Gilberto at the end of the mile-long road that led to the hotel exit. The area outside of our hotel was all tropical forest, so I felt like I was in the middle of nowhere. He drove us to a small, shack-like dwelling where he rented an ATV from a local. I learned that Costa Rican "businessmen" typically wear more than one hat. Our friendly ATV-rental guy was also the regional pimp, complete with a notebook full of local ladies of the night that he offered for rent by the hour.

We got onto the ATV and Gilberto whisked me away through the dense tropical forest, complete with monkeys in the trees. It was incredible. We saw a herd of 100 cattle pass us by, crossed little streams, and finally arrived at the cutest out-of-the-way bar hidden on the beach where we watched the sun set over the crystal blue ocean.

It was so romantic. Like a postcard—only we were in it!

Next, we hopped back on the ATV to head to Flamingo Beach, a popular tourist attraction because of its beautiful pink sand. This wasn't another quiet, picture-postcard encounter, though. Unless you like postcards featuring a fat, greasy, and shady-looking American guy standing on a tropical beach.

Turns out, the chubby American was a friend of Gilberto who owned a condo in the area. Because the sun had gone down and we were an hour-and-a-half of dense jungle away from my hotel, it looked like we would be bunking with Fatty for the night.

Of course, what fun is a double date with only one

girl? Before we could head for the condo, we had to pick up his friend's girlfriend.

At least, I thought she was his girlfriend.

We pulled up in front of a ramshackle old motel with a seediness level that was absolutely off the charts. There, to my complete surprise, out walked a *very* beautiful young woman.

It turned out that she wasn't his actual girlfriend. She was his girlfriend-for-the-night. Sort of like a pizza to go, only much, much hotter. I wondered if Fatty ordered her through the ATV guy's notebook.

I was a little freaked out. Here I was in a foreign country, in the middle of nowhere, an hour and a half from my hotel, with a man who had just picked up a hooker. This couldn't possibly be legal. What if we were pulled over? Never mind that—what if they were planning a whole new career for me?

My fears were calmed when we made it to Fatty's condo for some cocktails (I made mine a triple). We listened to music and just hung out, and the beautiful hooker turned out to be really nice. We all just chilled and I minded my Ps and Qs until Gilberto and I crashed in the spare bedroom.

The next morning, we watched the sun rise. It was my last Costa Rican sunrise. That was the day I was due to fly out—and for my tropical romance to come to an end.

Gilberto turned what could have been an ordinary trip into a real adventure. Even better, he was totally smitten with me. On one of our last nights, he got down on one knee and fake-proposed to me with a glass ring he bought on the beach. It was so sweet that he actually believed something could happen between us.

I blamed it on too much time in the sun and an abundance of cheap rum.

The reality is, you can't take the jungle out of the boy. Gilberto is a true native who needs his natural habitat to survive. For that matter, so do I! We still chat from time to time on Facebook, and it's always fun to look back on that amazing week.

Except the ant bites. Those I could forget.

Snaggle Tooth and Gay Bro

I took yet another trip with my man-magnet friend Zoe, this time to the sunshine of Spain and the island resort of Ibiza. In Ibiza, Miss Thing wound up with a dancer at one of the mega-clubs on the island. Of course, he was unbelievably hot. I woke up to her guy naked and asleep on our balcony, his bare ass visible to anyone lucky enough to look up. Me, I got stuck with a snaggle-tooth Italian guy. Nothing very memorable there.

Then, in Barcelona, it happened again! Zoe hooked up with an Australian who was quite a piece of eye candy and ran his own "female entertainment" business back in the Land of Oz. This time, I didn't even get a real date. I ended up chilling with his gay brother.

I had a much better experience in Barcelona when one of Zoe's sugar daddies picked us up on his yacht. He lives in Manhattan (and has a few houses scattered around the world), but he just happened to be in Spain at the same time we were. We were treated like royalty, jet setting around the Mediterranean in style, swimming in the warm water, and stopping on the shore for some haute seafood cuisine. I actually felt like I got the better end of the deal (for once!).

Sugar Daddy was over 60, so I was left to flirt with the only other person on board, the yacht's much younger (and more attractive) captain. We chatted and I caught some Mediterranean rays while Zoe disappeared down below deck for a while with the old man.

Excuse me while I throw up in my mouth.

Despite the perks of having a best girl with a Sugar Daddy, I realized that if meeting men was going to be a part of my travel experience, it was probably best if I left Zoe at home, not that I don't love her.

Luca Spaghetti

I had a chance to head down to Mexico for a three-day weekend in Riviera Maya. This time, I brought my friend Amber. We were in a club, where I was buzzed enough to be dancing on a couch or a table or some other piece of furniture, when I saw a guy peering up at me. Turns out he was from Italy (no snaggle tooth here), but living in Playa del Carmen. Apparently, my dancing made an impression on the boy. He must have had tequila goggles on, because I am a terrible dancer.

Two weeks later, he showed up on my doorstep in New York. Because he spoke zero English, I had a hard time determining how long he planned to stay… And exactly when he planned to leave! Don't get me wrong; he was a really nice guy with a heart of gold, but communicating with him was like playing a game of charades for five straight days. Plus, he smelled like Marlboro Reds, and since he snored like a buzz saw, sleeping together was a no-go. I kicked him to the couch after about four hours.

Manly Man

I recently won an award at work—and my prize was a trip anywhere in the world. With the entire globe at my disposal, I was able to choose a place I had always wanted to visit: Australia. I even got to add on a few days on the South Pacific island of Fiji.

This was a real dream trip—a trip of a lifetime. This time, I decided to go it alone. I had recently lost my father and needed some time to reflect and unwind. I pictured the trip as a kind of *Eat, Pray, Love* thing—only condensed into two weeks.

A friend of mine had taken a vacation to Sydney two months before I went, and she had a local boy picked out for me to meet because she knew I would be traveling solo and might get lonely. And I did. I booked five-star hotels because, since I was a woman traveling alone, I was worried about safety. (Plus, I deserved a little luxury!) But being alone in a luxury hotel full of couples and honeymooners and families can be kind of a bummer—even if you're attempting to recreate your own *Eat, Pray, Love* experience down under.

So I connected with the guy on Facebook and we made plans to meet on my third day in Sydney. He told me to bring my bikini and water, which sent me into a complete panic.

The bikini part; not the water part.

See, like ninety percent of women in the world, I'm self-conscious about my body, especially when ninety-five percent of that body is on display for anyone and everyone to see. I was a chubby kid who got picked on a lot, and while somewhere along the way I transformed from an ugly duckling into a swan, sometimes, inside, I still feel kind of like that duck.

So when I saw this amazing, perfect, model-gorgeous man walking up to ME—ME, there in my itsy-bitsy, teeny-weeny—my first thought was to turn around and run back inside the hotel. Or maybe pretend I spoke another language and didn't know who he was. I kept thinking, "OMG, I'm going to look like a beached whale next to this guy."

But I talked myself down from the ledge. After all, you only live once. Who knew if I would ever see him again? Sydney is about as far away from NYC as a person can get!

So I didn't run. I said hello, put a big, black bike helmet on, hopped on the back of his motorbike and we whisked through Sydney to catch the Manly Ferry for a day at the beach. I kept feeling my bikini bottoms creeping out of my sundress as we rode through the city and struggled to pull them back down to hide my butt. The Aussies commuting behind us were treated to quite a view of my American ass! I was also pinching myself the whole time because I felt so freakin' lucky to be in Australia, headed to a beautiful beach with such a beautiful Manly Man!

We found a secluded spot away from the tourists (Manly is a very popular destination) and just talked and talked for hours. We laughed, we played in the ocean, and eventually, we started flirting. I guess I didn't look that bad in my suit after all. Or maybe the sun had tanned me so much that I just looked skinnier. Either way, it was clear the sexual tension was building.

The ferry ride back to Sydney was breathtaking. He kissed me as the sun set over the Sydney Opera House—

probably one of the most romantic moments of my life. It felt like we had known each other a lot longer than a few hours.

We rode his bike back to my hotel. He came up to my room, and let's just say the lights went down. Then it was time to hit the town. He took me to his apartment overlooking Sydney Harbour—complete with an infinity pool. I kept asking myself, "Is this real? Who am I?" I felt so lucky—I couldn't wait to tell the girls back home!

The next stop on my trip was Queensland, and I was scheduled to go alone so I could reflect, get to know myself, grow as a person, and all that stuff.

But Manly Man kept dropping hints that he wanted to fly up to Queensland with me.

I kept blowing him off. I had planned this trip in a specific way for a specific reason. I wasn't getting a lot of that "quiet reflection" when all I was reflecting on was how amazingly awesome my new friend was.

But then I was kind of like, "*Why?*" This gorgeous, fun, nice guy was also so crazy-spontaneous that he would actually skip work to accompany a girl he just met on the next leg of her trip. I finally caved and said, "Yes! Book your ticket and come with me!" By then, it was too late. Lesson learned.

My final day in Sydney, Manly Man took me all over the city on his bike. He didn't want me to miss anything. We had wedges at the Opera House, we drove to the botanical gardens, we walked over the Harbour Bridge, we held hands, we kissed, and we enjoyed each other's company. In just two days, we had become great friends. We spent the last night in my hotel room, watching *Superman* and cuddling. It felt so good to be in the arms of a genuinely nice human being—not like most of the American boys I was used to dating.

Not to mention the fact that he is, hands down, the hottest and most down to earth guy I've ever been with— and he liked me!

Then, just as quickly as our adventure in Sydney had started, it was over. I actually cried at the airport as I boarded my plane to Queensland. I wondered, "Is this love?" Or was I just being my typical, foolish, romantic self?

Of course, my trip wasn't *all* about hooking up. I got in the best of both worlds and squeezed in as much culture and sightseeing as humanly possible in my short time down under. In Queensland, I had my picture taken next to a koala bear with big balls (my current Twitter picture if you're curious). I fed kangaroos, cruised down a crocodile infested river, and walked through the Daintree Rainforest (the oldest rainforest in the world—filled with lots of bugs, reptiles, and slithery things that can kill you). I went scuba diving at the Great Barrier Reef and hugged a sea turtle, and I went to Cape Tribulation (the only place in the world where two World Heritage sites meet). I really did it all.

Yes, in addition to a couple of guys. It was a very well rounded trip!

Hutches

The third stop on my journey was a quaint beach town near the very top of Australia called Port Douglas. Once again, all those families, newlyweds, and about-to-be newlyweds were constant reminders that I was ALONE.

I was sitting solo at the swim-up bar, nursing a drink

while watching the kids crawling all over the stools, when a guy approached me.

His friends called him "Hutches." He was a Kiwi (what New Zealanders call themselves) who was in town for a friend's wedding. I never found out why they call him Hutches. Maybe he was known for inventing that type of furniture or something. Who knows? Anyway, Hutches definitely was not my tall, dark, and handsome type—he was a little goofy-looking, but at that point I was desperate to talk with anyone, and he was single and nice. So why not? We had a few laughs, and eventually I met the other guys in the wedding party and even the groom-to-be.

We all hung out at a cute little bar across from the ocean—it was like a bachelor party, and I was like one of the guys. The groom even invited me to come to the wedding. I would be off to Fiji by then, so I had to decline, but it would have been fun.

Still—only I would be invited to a wedding while on holiday on the other side of the earth!

Anyway, back to the bar. I think I tried every slushy, fruity beverage on the menu, which must have put my total to at least six. By that time, I had developed a serious case of beer goggles. Or tropical drink goggles, which, considering the strength of those beverages, had to be worse. I didn't want to walk (or stumble) back to my hotel all alone. I guess I just didn't want the evening to end quite so soon. So I decided to let Hutches the Kiwi escort me back to my hotel.

Then I invited him up to my suite.

Let me be clear: I had no intention of hooking up with him. None whatsoever! It's just that, after a few days of listening to nothing but the screams of kids in the pool and the smooches of young lovers, I wanted some human conversation. Plus, I had this amazing hot tub on my balcony that I hadn't made use of yet, because what fun is a hot tub when you're alone?

So we went into the hot tub in bathing suits and poured every single shampoo and body wash I could find in my suite into the tub. We cracked open the free bottle of wine the hotel sent me after I complained that the Wi-Fi wasn't working, and we had an absolute blast! There were bubbles everywhere—we could barely see each other through all the foam. We were laughing and drinking and felt like high rollers, living it up in a hot tub on the balcony of a fancy-schmantzy hotel suite.

I felt so free being halfway across the planet from home, having the most amazing time. BUT—not free enough to hook up with poor Hutches. Of course, he kept asking, but I kept pushing him away until he got the hint. He wound up crashing in my room and left the next day. No sex, but still one of the most memorable nights of my life!

Miner Jeffrey

My final destination on this trip was Fiji—and I was more than a little excited to get there. Ever since I was a little girl, I always dreamed of running away to Fiji. It was about as far away from Long Island as any place I could imagine. Now, I was actually doing it. Okay, it was only for five days, but still!

Fiji did not disappoint. Out of all of my travels, it is my favorite place in the world. The locals are amazing! I permanently have the words "*Bula Bula Bula*" ingrained in my brain. *Bula* means "hello," but it also means "a life is walking toward you," so when you say "*Bula*," you greet life. At least, that's what one of the older Fijians I met told me, but maybe he was just high on too much kava (a Fijian treat that's kind of like marijuana in beverage form).

I drank kava, too, with the chief of a village I visited. I also went scuba diving, and saw a cave where cannibalism was practiced as recently as the eighteenth century. And I fell in love with the people of Fiji, who are the happiest people on earth—some of them even live off the land with no electricity or running water. The high school children in one village near the cannibal cave swim across the river every day to get to school! Such a simple, beautiful life.

But, again, at my fancy resort packed with couples on romantic vacations (and families dealing with the after-effects of too much romance), I felt a little lonely. So I decided to plant myself at the adult pool at the resort (no more screaming children who were probably peeing in the pool, please!) and wait at the swim-up bar for anyone I could try to socialize with.

It worked! Instead of hooking up with another guy, this time I met an awesome group of girls from Australia there for a girls' vacay. No, not like *that!* These were girls who like boys, just like me, and before long a group of adorable Australian boys had joined us at the swim-up bar.

The girls were leaving the following day, but just my luck, the boys weren't. The guys were there for their best friend's wedding, which he had cancelled at the last minute after everyone had already flown to the island. Apparently the bridegroom reached the decision that he wasn't ready to get married—something all of his friends already agreed about. So everyone was in the mood to party it up, and party we did!

Miner Jeffrey was one of the guys in the wedding party, and proved to be my personal knight in shining armor for this final leg of my trip. He was over six feet tall with an amazing body, probably from his work in the mines in Australia.

Let's just say he was very good with his hands.

But back to my story. The guys in this group really were boys—at least compared to me at the ripe old age of thirty-one. Miner Jeffrey told me he was twenty-nine, but when I noticed his email address ended in the number eighty-seven, I asked if that might possibly represent his birth year. He was adorable when he finally admitted that yes, he was really twenty-six. He blushed and said he thought a mature, adult woman like me wouldn't want to talk to him if I knew how young he was.

Apparently, they've never heard of cougars in Australia, not that I'm anywhere near close to cougar-hood yet.

Miner Jeffrey and I spent the next two days together just as Mr. Manly and I did in Sydney. Of course, after my balcony bubble bath in Port Douglas, we just had to fill the tub with every soap-like product that the room offered. Afterward, let's just say he filled the slippers and bathrobe that came with my hotel suite very nicely!

We swapped stories of our lives back home in our native countries—dating, work, our families, travels, and more. We drank on my balcony in our slippers and robes until the wee hours of the morning dancing, laughing, and listening to the waves of the Pacific crashing on the beach. It was very therapeutic—almost like the luxury hotel room came with a nice, sweet, sexy guy as an amenity. Not that I saw him as a thing. Two days with him felt like weeks with the guys I date back home. We really got to know each other.

For my final night in Fiji—and of my entire South Pacific adventure—I trekked across the sand to Miner Jeffrey's simpler, no-frills resort for a kava ceremony. There were Fijians, Miner Jeffrey and his friends, and some other travelers all sitting around in a circle on the floor, listening to the kava guy play his little guitar and sing.

It was a magical ending to a magical trip!

I felt so alive, so amazing, and so fortunate to have made so many good friends from all around the world. Who would have thought a girl like me from Suffolk County would be sitting in freakin' paradise? The hotel staff even sang me a goodbye song and wished me well on my travels home back across the world.

Of course, me being me, I cried.

After the ceremony, we took a cab to meet the rest of the guys in the non-wedding party at another resort. I met all of MJ's closest friends who had also flown in from the land down under, and they were all wonderful people. I also heard the story of how the almost-groom dodged a bullet by not getting married. Apparently, all of his friends and family were elated that he didn't go through with it. He must have been twenty-four or twenty-five—way too young, I think, to even consider getting married, although he was practically an old man compared to me when I walked down the aisle. I shared my own story and my best "older-woman" advice about waiting until the time and the person are right.

Think of everything I would have missed if I had settled for less.

We talked for a while and drank yummy cocktails, and then we all jumped into the pool that bordered the South Pacific Ocean.

Before I knew it, the sun was coming up over Miner Jeffrey's glimmering back muscles and my enchanted holiday was over. Damn, they do make them good in Oz! I didn't want the moment to end because I knew that in twenty-four hours I would be back in the real world.

However, all three of the guys I met on my Australian odyssey still stay in touch with me. The magic of Facebook!

Now why can't any guy from my homeland be so good at communicating?

What I learned on the road:

- Live in the moment or you might have some regrets later. I may never stop kicking myself for stopping Manly Man from following me to Queensland!

- Don't over analyze—just go with it. Not just in dating, but at work, with friends, and in daily life.

- Travelling alone is awesome—it takes you out of your comfort zone and forces you to experience new things and meet new people.

- We're all kids at heart, so fill up a tub and have a bubble bath with a friend!

Eight
Serial Dating Survival

For me, a return to the real world meant a return to my life of serial dating.

"Serial Dating" is my term for going out on at least two or more first dates per week. It's a vicious cycle that's part of the online dating experience—the whole point of online dating is to meet a guy you can have a relationship with, but finding the right guy usually means a lot of first dates with a lot of different prospects.

The problem is, most of the guys you're serial dating are also checking out *their* options, which means even if you have a great time and feel like you've made a connection, there's no guarantee Date One will lead to Date Two.

The result is something like Groundhog Day. You ask the exact same questions. "Where are you from?" "What do you do?" "Where did you go to school?" You answer the exact same questions about yourself. Over, and over, and over again. It starts to feel like interviewing for a job, except the job title is "girlfriend."

All those nights out, all those déjà vu conversations—

it can be exhausting and a little depressing. It's even fattening: Serial dating usually means at least two dinners out a week, plus drinks, meaning you wake up the next day feeling too tired to move.

I can only handle serial dating for a couple of months at a time before I have to retreat back to the quiet and safety of my apartment. Some days I feel like giving up hope dating in NYC, but other days the urge to meet Mr. Right never completely goes away, so I've come up with a few rules to try to make the process easier.

First, if I need to be at work the next day, I tell the guy I turn into a pumpkin at midnight. That means I'll be rested for work, less likely to overeat (being tired and hungover tends to wear on my will power), and, most importantly, I don't have to pay for a taxi. I won't take the subway after about 11:30 at night, and all those cab fares during a serial dating binge can add up.

I have another even more important survival tactic—one that helps me maintain my figure and pay my rent.

Let me explain.

My friends and I live in New York City, which, in case you haven't heard, is one of the most expensive places on the planet to call home. My friend Rose came up with a way to transform the sometimes-depressing chore of serial dating into a productive enterprise.

I call it "Serial Dating on a Budget."

Here's how it works.

As I already mentioned, most first dates involve having dinner. The majority of the time (unless you've gone out with some of the winners I have), the man pays. Certainly in the beginning, anyway.

Just because he pays for the food doesn't mean you have to eat everything on your plate, however.

(Even if your mother told you that you did.)

Any week when I have at least two dates planned, I'll start the evening with a martini with bleu cheese stuffed olives. They're like an appetizer and they make it a whole lot easier to leave a substantial portion of my dinner on my plate.

Now I am NOT one of those girls who are afraid to let a guy know she likes to eat. I think food is one of the great pleasures in life, and why would I deny myself pleasure? When I'm serial dating, however, it's a little different. If I don't eat everything on my plate, I can take whatever's left home in a doggy bag. Suddenly, instead of worrying about the cost of cab fare home, I'm saving money on lunch the next day!

My friend Rose has this down to a science. The girl hasn't bought herself lunch in over a year.

The key, for me, is beverages. You can't take those home with you, so feel free to indulge. If martinis with stuffed olives aren't your thing, wine spritzers or other carbonated drinks are good—the bubbly sensation will fill up your tummy.

A couple of those and you'll be so full; you won't even be able to think about the half chicken (or eight-ounce T-bone, or steaming plate of pasta) sitting in front of you.

Until lunchtime tomorrow, that is.

Over time, you'll find your grocery bills diminishing, so for every date that doesn't pan out, you'll still have something tangible to show for time spent.

Maybe you can even doggie bag your way to a new outfit or an amazing pair of shoes!

You can wear them on your next serial date, which might look something like this…

Nine
One-Date Wonders

"But Mary," you may be protesting after reading that last chapter, "can these dates really be so bad that the only thing that makes them bearable is the possibility of a free, chef-prepared lunch?"

Ohhhhhhh, they can.

Keep in mind that the following are just a few examples out of the many, many, MANY first date nightmares I have personally experienced.

Turkish Rose

The following is one of the most important pieces of advice you will receive in this whole, entire book.

Ready?

Do not, I repeat, do NOT go out on a date with someone you meet online without first speaking with him on the phone.

How do I know? Because of the man (and I use the term loosely) I nicknamed Turkish Rose.

I connected with Turkish Rose on OkCupid. He was

articulate and intelligent in print, so I assumed the in-person version would offer more of the same. I knew he was Turkish; I love Turkish food, so we arranged to meet at a Turkish restaurant. When I spotted him across the street from our destination, I thought this date might go well. He was dressed like a hipster—something different for me! Maybe he was the artsy type! Maybe this date could actually be fun!

Maybe the ninety-degree heat and the fact that I just hauled ass all the way from work to the East Side to meet him in my business suit rendered me temporarily insane!

When I saw my date up close, all those maybes were replaced with one very large word: RUN! In front of me stood a man so slight, so petite, that if you glanced at him quickly (and maybe without your glasses) he bore a striking resemblance to Audrey Hepburn.

And not in a good way.

Eying this wisp of a man with little twiggy legs who I swear was half my size, I suggested we get a drink before dinner. I needed time to size up the situation before I committed to an entire two-hour meal with this man. He agreed, and took me to a bar that closely resembled a dungeon. Just to make the steamy, summer evening extra special, the bar had no A/C.

Great. Just give me the bottle; no straw required.

When we sat down, I couldn't help noticing the delicate way he crossed his legs. Just like a very proper woman. Then I tried to start a conversation, and discovered getting a complete sentence out of him was like pulling teeth.

Why? Because he was totally stoned!

When I asked what he did after work, his response was, "I spoke a joint." Yes, you read that correctly: "spoke."

"Every day?" I asked. He responded with one word, "Yes." Clearly, he had "spoken," and rather heavily, before our date.

That was enough for me. My longed-for Turkish dinner would have to wait—it was time to hatch an escape plan. I ran to the bathroom, called my roommate Gwen, and asked her to call me in fifteen minutes and tell me there was a flood in our apartment and I had to come home.

She did. I think she even said the cats were drowning.

That was the end of my date with my Turkish Rose. He was never to be seen or heard from again. However, he did cross my mind the other night when I was watching *Breakfast at Tiffany's.*

No, the Audrey Hepburn look just doesn't work on a man.

Insufficient Funds

I've already shared a few stories from the pit of dating hell known as Match.com, but this particular one-date wonder is one of my personal favorites. It began with my very first glimpse of my latest "catch" wearing a shimmering suit that was two sizes two small and a mouth that was too sizes too big. He looked a little like a used car salesman from the "outer boroughs" (Outer Mongolia, to be exact).

Of course, looks aren't everything, so I fought the impulse to run in the opposite direction and instead decided on a Thai restaurant. At this point, my companion for the evening revealed the fact that he had spent a whopping $250 on lunch that day (maybe that explained why his suit was so small?). But that's not the best part. Apparently, this midday delight was held at the zoo, where the soon-to-be-entrees paraded across the table in front of the guests before they were skewered and served.

Just imagine how this tidbit whetted my appetite.

However, despite the fact that he'd consumed $250 worth of defenseless zoo animals a few hours prior, my date had plenty of room for more inside that tiny, shiny suit. He proceeded to order up a veritable Thai feast and slurp it down with all of the grace and dignity of a POW who hadn't been fed in a month.

I felt a little queasy. Not to mention panicked that someone I knew might spot me with my latest "match." Hoping to put a quick and painless end to what felt like a very long and painful evening, I offered to split the bill for our date.

"I won't hear of it," Insufficient Funds replied as he wiped food residue from his face, and immediately slapped his credit card on the table.

It was declined.

Three times.

(I guess the nickname was kind of a dead giveaway.)

The waitress helpfully suggested he might want to try the local ATM, located right on the corner. He went to do just that—and left me at the restaurant for a good twenty minutes. When he got back—surprise!—Insufficient Funds had no more cash than when he left. "Maybe," he suggested, "the machine is broken?"

I looked at him as if he was an escapee from the local mental institution. He showed me the ATM receipt. I calmly explained that the receipt showed that he had no money in his account.

While in my head, I was thinking, "NO CASH! NO

DINERO, CHARLIE! THAT'S RIGHT, YOU ASSHOLE! YOU'RE TAPPED OUT!!"

I asked him how he could possibly show up for a first date under such dire financial straits, and why he didn't just go Dutch from the start rather than offer to pay the whole thing from the get-go. That led right into the best part of this entire nightmare evening.

Insufficient Funds very serenely explained that this was his practice on first dates just to see how "potential girl-friends" will react.

Let's just say that didn't go over well with this "potential girlfriend."

I completely lost it. Anyone listening might have thought I was the spawn of pirates. What I remember was something along the lines of, "Are you fucking kidding me? You asked me to choose a restaurant and I did. You declined my offer to split the bill. And all the while you showed up without a dime?"

I'm pretty sure there was more. I blocked the rest of the experience out.

However, there is a happy-ish ending to this story: Prince Charming did give me a ride home, and the next week he sent me a check for his half of the dinner bill.

And it didn't bounce!

However, my auto pay to Match.com will bounce from that moment until the end of time.

Gelato

Zap! That nasty little bastard cherub from OkCupid hit me with another one of his poison arrows (he looks so innocent and inviting on the webpage). The only thing good about my experience with Gelato was that he ended up being a one-date wonder. Had he not, my apartment might have become a crime scene.

I met Gelato at a little place by the same name near Central Park. His opening remarks sounded compelling enough: He was a professional athlete who moved back to New York to care for a sick family friend. He was a bit loud and brash, but claimed it was just his style to speak his mind and "keep it real, ya know."

Anyway, the beginning and end of our short little tale goes like this: During the consumption of our refreshing gelato and the ensuing walk, we talked about everything from cooking to travel and more. Because we seemed to have some chemistry, I broke my own rule and invited him over to my apartment for dinner a few days later.

The text exchange that follows ensured that second date never happened. (Please excuse any typos, as this is the actual, unedited exchange of messages.):

ME: Just bring yourself and a bottle of something if u want.

GEL: *Do I need condoms?*

ME: No. This is a friendly dinner. BTW, are u serious about that comment?

GEL: *So we hanging out?*

ME: I thought that was the plan?

GEL: *So what do I bring?*

ME: I said a bottle of something.

ME: Do u want to hang out?

GEL: *Do I get a lap dance?*

ME: I'll pole dance (Dear Reader, obviously I was kidding with this text.)

GEL: *What else?*

GEL: *Do I need condoms?*

ME: No!

GEL: *Why u don't use them?*

ME: We r not having sex.

GEL: *U sure... I wanna be ready in case.*

ME: I can't tell if you're joking or not? I'm not inviting u over for that intention, so if that's what you're looking for then maybe dinner on 2nd date is not a good idea...

GEL: *Ha ha*

ME: Please let me know so I'm not wasting my time.

GEL: *Oh man...Ur so serious*

ME: It is very hard to read u over txt. And even though I started preparing, before I go any further, please let me know what I should do.

GEL: *Sorry. I don't think we mix well.*

ME: Okay then. That's fine. Wish I would have known be-

fore I went and bought everything.

GEL: U seem serious

ME: Huh?

GEL: U seem serious

ME: What do u mean?

ME: U asked if you could bring condoms over. I couldn't tell if that was a joke or not.

GEL: I feel ur uptight

ME: U don't even know me. And it's hard to read via text. Put yourself in my shoes too. I thought I would stray from the norm and invite a guy over I met once for dinner!

GEL: Yea

ME: I'm such a fool!

GEL: How u figure?

ME: I was looking forward to getting to know u. Went and got all this stuff and NOW u tell me u don't think we mix?

GEL: U seem serious

GEL: Are u wearing panties tonite?

ME: Maybe you're right. Maybe we don't mix well.

ME: I stopped cooking. Going out now! Good luck!

GEL: Thanks...u too.

In the end, I happily shared my feast with my girl Jaclyn and her boyfriend from down the block. They were much better dinner companions—and as far as I know, neither of them brought condoms.

Chucky Cheese

I am giving my friend Cher her own personal entry in the One-Date Wonders chapter because her story is too funny to pass up! Cher met the guy we call Chucky Cheese on Tinder. Unbeknownst to Cher, the venue where Chucky told Cher to meet him was a Chuck E. Cheese's-like establishment in Queens—he even brought his two small children along for the fun! Chucky showed up sporting a polo shirt with lines and stripes going every direction to the point where they could induce a seizure, shorts, white socks pulled up to his knees, and Converse sneakers. They dined on the finest chicken fingers and French fries and washed it down with a vintage 2014 Co-ca-Cola. Cher may as well have been in the Midwest and not in Queens, NY! He should have just told her to meet him at McDonald's.

What I learned from my one-date wonders:

- Have at least one phone conversation before meeting. More on this in Chapter 13.

- Don't offer to cook dinner for a guy on a second date. Learn his true colors before you spend your hard-earned money and waste a Friday night.

- Run if your date wears socks up to his knees and asks you to meet him at a venue that caters mostly to the under-five set.

- If you know there will not be a second date before the first is even over (or started) you've probably saved yourself a lot of time that would be better spent watching trash TV and drinking wine with girlfriends. Consider THAT a win. ☺

Ten

Vanishing Acts

Vanishing Acts are kind of the opposite of One-Date Wonders: They're the guys you think you're going to have a second (or first, or third, or whatever) date with, you think you have chemistry, you think all the nice things they're saying are true…

Then they just disappear. Poof.

Every woman who's ever dated in her life has probably encountered at least one Vanishing Act in one form or another. It happens more often than that in New York, probably because there are so many people living in the city—a good guy might have several options to consider. He might have amazing chemistry with Girl One, but wonder what might happen with Girl Two. So he vanishes on Girl One and moves on to Girl Two, until Girl Three comes along. It's a dizzying cycle.

Here are a few of my most memorable mystery men…

Newton

Newton is a Vanishing Act who never ventured past the initial email phase—something that happens all too frequently with guys you meet online. You seem to have a connection, they seem to want to get together, but it never happens and, eventually, they vanish.

I met Newton on OkCupid and we had awesome email exchanges that included some real, actual conversation. He finally asked for my number so he could call and take our conversation offline. And he never called. End of Vanishing Act. I have had at least a 100 Newtons, and I'm sure some of you ladies reading this have had a few Newtons as well.

Apollo

Apollo is a rarity in my life: an actual, flesh-and-blood male whom I met in real life and not online. My girlfriends and I stumbled into a bar after going into a seedy sex shop on 8th Avenue for shits and giggles. We all squeezed into one of those porno video booths—it was a little crazy—and promptly got kicked out because apparently only one pervert is allowed in the booth at a time! So we were still laughing our heads off when we walked into the bar next door and I met Apollo.

We started chatting it up and we discovered we're actually neighbors—he only lives one block away from me, which I thought was pretty convenient. I was leaving for my vacation in Australia in a week, and Apollo said he wanted to take me out to dinner when I got back. He also said I was "unlike other girls," "beautiful," and had a "good head on my shoulders." He even posed the age-old question, "Why are you still single?" So many of the guys I meet ask this particular question. I never know when it's heartfelt or a bunch of BS, so I usually don't get my hopes up.

Still, it certainly sounded like he was interested.

However, it's been months since I returned from the land down under, and unless a miracle occurs while this book is being printed, I still haven't gotten that dinner date. All I've gotten are a bunch of lame texts, including the "hope you had fun" he sent when I let him know I was back in town and the occasional 3:00 a.m. drunk text asking, "what's up?"

Delete!

Harley

Harley is probably the worst kind of Vanishing Act: The kind that vanishes in the middle of what seems to be a developing relationship. Or at least a developing *something*. I met him on How About We and we had two fantastic dates. At least I thought they were fantastic. Maybe I should have paid a little bit more attention to the fact that, on the second date, he'd forgotten everything I told him about myself on the first. He didn't remember what I did for a living, or where I lived. We were having so much fun, I didn't think much of it. Maybe he just had a bad memory.

On the other hand, maybe he was getting me mixed up with the seventeen other dates he had between our first and our second.

Anyway, we made out, went out to dinner, held hands, went to a fancy private speakeasy—it was a great, fun evening. He went out of town for a few days, but we stayed in touch via text (how did we ever date before technology?). He kept telling me how much he was looking forward to seeing me when he got back to NYC.

I'm still waiting for that third date.

Maybe he just never came home?

James Bond

James was a Vanishing Act of the lengthier variety, possibly because we met at the annual hotel conference held by the company where I worked at the time. James was the corporate group sales director for the sister property right next door—what a coincidence! When I would take my well-deserved breaks from convincing guests to attend our time-share presentations (as mentioned in Rico Suave), I would stroll over to the Starbucks in James's hotel hoping to casually bump into him.

And what do you know? On my third attempt, we actually bumped! That's when the flirting started.

James is South African, and you already know I'm always a sucker for a guy with an accent. He was also easy on the eyes, in his early forties, and had played football (the European kind) in his early years. After I was lucky enough to be seated next to him at the company holiday party, I was hooked. I took our seating arrangements as a sign that our flirty coffee break conversations were going to be bumped up to the next level.

The only problem? He was married.

Actually, as he told me when we went out for happy hour after the party, he was separated. Because he and his wife had many assets tied up together, the divorce was a very slow process, so we decided to be "just friends" instead.

We emailed several times a week for a couple of months. Then I left my "glamorous" hotel gig and his emails stopped. He just disappeared. I emailed him numerous times, but there was no reply.

WTF?

This Vanishing Act actually has a Part Two. About two

years after he vanished, I got an email from him using the name "James Bond" (as opposed to his real name, which I am not using here). He said he had moved back to South Africa to try to get his divorce finalized, and that he was back in the States and wanted to see me. He was renting a room in a house a Long Island Railroad ride away in Franklin Square.

Because I had known him for a couple of years, I let the fact that he was living in Long Island slide.

We hung out a few times, always ending up at my place because he didn't have money to spend. Turns out he was trying to get his new business off the ground—which he apparently co-owned with his wife. WTF yet again! I thought he was getting a divorce.

We started emailing again on a daily basis because he "couldn't" give me his cell phone number. Weird. He said it was his work cell and his wife was on the account. They didn't live together, so what difference would it have made?

Anyway, here is a *condensed* version of our email exchanges, so you can get an up-close and personal look at the Vanishing Act at its finest.

February, 2013

JB: Hey Mary... How have you been? Not sure if you remember me. :)

ME: Well, hello there. It's been a very long time! Of course, I remember you. What have you been up to? Still in NYC?

JB: It would take a looong happy hour to tell you what has been going on. I have been in South Africa (still here) for the last ten months sorting out all my crap. Moving back to New York middle-March finally. My divorce goes through in August (have been separated for almost a year), and after a whole lot of money wasted and time, my new life starts (I know you have been through this before). So, looking for a job when I arrive, maybe real estate, I will see.

What have you been up to? How is life treating you??

ME: I'm still trying to figure out why your email comes up as "James Bond"? Sounds like you've been through battle but have successfully come out alive. I'm planning a trip to South Africa in October. I wouldn't say "wasted money" because you can't really put a price tag on sanity and being happy (although money does help).

It is a start to a new chapter in your life, which should be very exciting and liberating.

I'm working for a management company and have been here for about two years. I feel like a therapist most of the time!

Other than work and running around the city with friends, I continue to go on terrible first dates, lol!

It's nice to hear from you.

JB: My email James Bond is the email I used when I was going back and forth with my attorneys. They loved it. :) I actually like that name better than mine. :) That's great that you have settled into a position you would be great at. If they have any jobs coming up, let me know. :)

It would be great to see you again when I get to

NY, and also have the odd email chat. :) I will give you a heads up where and what places to go to when you visit South Africa.

ME: Maybe you should change your name legally to James Bond and really start over!! It has a sexy tone to it... James Bond... Very double-0-7. ;)

We definitely need a proper happy hour upon your return.

JB: Hopefully I will be over there earlier. I was sure you would have yourself a fine young man by now. Especially the way you look. :)

ME: One encounters a lot of frogs living in NYC when it comes to dating.

JB: Can't sleep.... I think I'm slipping back to US times zone.

That was funny. :) You can afford to wait for Mr. Right with your looks. :)

I have to go to Chicago soon to get certified for a part of my business. I was thinking I would love to spend a night in NY. I will confirm dates if you are around and you have time.

Nice chatting. :)

ME: Yes, let me know when you're around NY. I will be here and look forward to catching up after you disappeared... Just kidding.

JB: I promise when we go out for a drink it WILL be happy hour. :) I used to want to do everything such as work, play, drink as if I only had minutes to live, but I am more at peace with myself and ENJOYING everything day by day.

I don't have specific dates, but will let you know when I touch down in the US... Soon.

JB: *I think I will be in Manhattan in about two weeks. Probably on a Thursday at this stage.*

ME: *I'll make sure to cancel all of my hot dates to squeeze you in.*

JB: *I'm thinking now that it's going to be too hard for next Thursday night. I finish off Friday anyway so I'm going to head to NY after that.... FOR GOOD. So let ALL your boyfriends know they don't have to piss off that Thursday. :)*

March

JB: *Ok... I am going to ask you a question and the answer will not change anything. I am moving in with a friend in Nassau County, Long Island. I arrive on Monday, but I can't move in until Thursday!!!! I will pay good money to sleep on your floor. Now Mary... I'm serious. Not being sleazy. Will still get drunk with you.*

JB: *Actually Mary.... Maybe my last email not a good idea. At airport, will call you when I arrive in Chicago. What's your cell number?*

ME: *You're confusing me. I don't think it's a good idea to crash here, you're right. I thought you were flying to*

Chicago then flying back to SA then flying to NY mid-March to move here?

JB: I will be in town Thursday. Do you want me to call then? If you're not busy, maybe happy hour drinks?

ME: I'm confused! Happy hour would be nice but I feel you have a lot going on so if you need to get settled back into life here first before meeting up that's fine too. Let me know what you want to do or I'll make other plans for Thursday.

JB: Ok... We can do it next week if you like? No stress at all.

ME: I'm totally confused. Are you staying in Chicago 'til Thursday? Then Thursday moving to Long Island?

<u>JB is finally back in the states</u>

JB: Sorry... I'm in Chicago now and have organized an apt in Franklin Square. I'm totally cool if you want to do something next week.

ME: Where is Franklin Square, lol? Let's play Thursday by ear.

JB: I'm back for good baby. :) This is my thought when we catch up.... Because I'm broke for the next few months, when we catch up let's do the happy hour thing (your recommendation) and then grab some beer, pizza, wine, and relax. And of course, no funny business. This divorce cost me a bomb... But who cares.... If you want to do something else, let me know.

ME: It'll be nice to have a new friend. No funny business.

JB: *I don't want to give you the impression that when we catch up for a drink that I want to just get you in bed!!! I'm saying that I find you very, very attractive. :) But let's have some drinks and relax and I will promise I will go home. :)*

ME: I don't get too drunk on a school night, FYI. I turn into a pumpkin after midnight. On the weekend, it's anyone's game!

JB: *OK! Maybe an afternoon session?*

ME: Afternoon? We will figure it out. No need to get stupid sloppy drunk! I want to remember our conversation.

JB: *FYI, there is no rebound here. It's been 12 months. But...after all this time there is an attraction towards you! Strange. :) But I am so relaxed. If something happens, it happens. If it doesn't...Good friends. :)*

ME: Do you have a cell phone yet?

JB: *No. I have an iPhone but it's connected to my wife's account. She says she would never check it. I say pig's ass you wouldn't...*

ME: Thought you were divorced?

JB: *Separated. I will be divorced once we agree on house, car, and business.*

At this point, we finally got together...

JB: Hey babe.... Thank you for a fantastic night!! I hope we can do this again soon. :) You are so funny and smart and you hit all the right buttons with me. :) Enjoy your day, and I'm sorry I kept you up too late. And hope I didn't snore too much??

And later that day...

JB: For me it is not just my physical attraction I have for you but it's the mental connection also... I'm sitting here eating lunch and my cock is still hard thinking about it. :)

ME: Ha ha. Agreed. You're making me blush!

One week later...

JB: Ok... This what I'm thinking babe... You're a little curious about me, and about my split with wifey. You think I'm going to go around and spread my seeds. Here is the story... I have been doing that for almost 12 months. I like you, and that's why I touched base, but now I'm thinking you are on the dating websites looking for your Mr. Right, which is fine. Maybe you should go and sort that out and then contact me... I'm cool with this. :)

ME: Where is this coming from? I really don't understand what your email means? You initially suggested we are friends, and I thought we were friends, getting to know each other (finally). And if you like me, why would you want me to go on dating websites? I like you, too!! Just want to take things slow... We only hung out two times!

Two years ago and this recent time. I was very happy you got in touch with me – I always wondered what happened to you. But I'm not understanding your passive aggressive tone referring to me dating and sorting things out? I have been dating for five years and def. do not need to find Mr. Right and rush into anything with anyone just to be with somebody. I'm not desperate to find Mr. Right. I have always been very independent and if Mr. Right comes along now or 10 years from now I'm cool with it, ha ha!

Just be straight up and tell me what you're thinking because I'm confused.

Thanks!

JB: *Ok babe... I arrived here three weeks ago. You told me that I'm playing the field. Or something... I have done this – a long time ago! I don't know what else to say.*

ME: I understand.

JB: *That's good... So you understand that I like you, and I hope you feel the same!!*

Later that day…

ME: How do you conduct a business with no phone?

JB: *No... I have phone for business. I'm just being careful. I will give it to you tonight.*

The next day…

JB: Had another good night babe. :)

About two weeks later…

JB: I'm traveling from tomorrow all week. Last minute. Let's catch up when I'm back.

ME: Where are you traveling to? Let's get together when you're back.

<u>April</u>

JB: Hey, I have to go to South Africa for a couple of weeks. I'm leaving Monday. Returning from Kentucky tomorrow morning. It would be great to see you before I go?

ME: Why are you traveling so much – is it for work? Tomorrow works. Want to grab dinner?

JB: Ok... Landing in morning. Chat then. Can you come to Long Island? I can pick you up.

ME: Pick me up? Do you drive? It would be nice for me to get off the island of Manhattan for a while so I will dust off my passport and ride the iron horse under the East River to visit. :) Do I get to see where you live?

JB: Babe I'm flying back this afternoon now. Won't get home until 9:30, which is ok but leaving for airport tomorrow at 7am. I will email you when I arrive and see if we can meet. Maybe if you get the bus out to LaGuardia airport and I pick u up? But I can't have a late one.

ME: Bummer! That's kind of late, I was hoping to meet up much earlier. I thought your stop was Franklin Square? Why would I go to LaGuardia? Let's plan to hang when you're back in the States again when we don't have to rush around. Why are you traveling so much?

JB: Hey babe.... Work. At airport now. It was a last minute thing with both trips...it will be like this for a little bit.

ME: When are you back from SA? Don't forget me. ;)

JB: I won't forget you. :) See you when I'm back.

Two weeks later…

JB: Hey Mary.... Sorry for the delayed response. It is love-ly down here. Heading up to Cape Town this morning for meetings. Been really busy which is good. How are you doing?

ME: I'm doing well. I got so used to your emails I guess I was having withdrawal.

<u>May</u>

ME: Guess there is no Internet in South Africa.

Three weeks later…

ME: Hey there – How are you? What's your deal? I haven't heard from you in over a month. This is not cool.... Is everything okay?

JB: *Hi Mary.... Sorry for not getting back to you. Things got really messy over here. Will be back in a few months.*

ME: *I can still be a friend.*

I never heard from him again.

No goodbye, no explanation, no nothing. That is the thing about a vanishing act. They disappear from your life, but they never totally disappear from your mind.

They don't have the decency to let you move on.

Then again, maybe he was kidnapped by aliens or something. Or swallowed by a great white shark. I've heard South Africa is known for sharks.

What my vanishing acts have taught me:

- As the old saying goes, talk is cheap and actions speak louder than words.

- If he won't give you his cell number, he most likely will not be giving you an engagement ring either.

- Sometimes, guys are just dicks. End of story.

Eleven

Lip Slut

With all these years in the dating trenches under my belt, I realized it was time for some New Rules (shout out to Bill Maher):

I will no longer sleep with anyone on the first, second, or even the "magical" third date. After Burak, I quickly learned that holding out as long as possible allows you to become more comfortable with each other and not feel like a total slut if they bail later on in the "relationship" or courting phase. I've managed to stick to this rule... More or less.

Why? Because—reality! Sweating up the sheets with someone so early in the game never goes anywhere. Of course, holding out until the sixth date never goes anywhere, either, but for some reason it just feels better this way.

But when you're attracted to a new guy, and the attraction is mutual, you've still got to do *something* to release the tension. I've solved this sticky problem by relegating my carnal activities to varying degrees of lip locking.

Hence the term "Lip Slut."

Don't bother to check Webster's, as it isn't in there—yet. So allow me to define it here: *Lip Slut*

English, USA
Noun
Definition: Someone who just wants to make out and nothing else.

If you're currently in the midst of a serial dating binge, I highly recommend this activity. Once you try it and get a little practice, you'll be surprised at the erotic satisfaction that can be derived through the experience. Although, admittedly, my dates haven't always mirrored my enthusiasm. But you know what, ladies? That's just tough. There's a new sheriff in town and I've decided after years on the "campaign trail" that it's my—and our—turn to call the shots.

At least we have our dignity, if nothing else, locked in.

I've gotten so good at Lip Slut-hood (or is it Lip Slut-dom?), at this point, I could easily compete for a gold medal in the Olympics—if they only recognized this delicately honed skill as the athletic feat it is.

Naturally, if a viable candidate pops up on the horizon, I am not averse to lifting the "above the neck restriction," but in the meantime, I've been told I'm a very good kisser!

These lucky winners might be able to tell you more.

Frenchie

I was visiting a friend in Boston when I met a French guy (hence the nickname) who was on vacation. He was foreign, which always appeals to me, and couldn't speak a lick of English, which occasionally appeals to me even more. So much drinking and lip locking ensued. Maybe, in retrospect, a little too much drinking.

The next thing I remember, after the make out session, is me in a drunken stupor, dragging poor Frenchie around a strange city in a quest to find something familiar. Finally, I managed to locate my friend's condo. Jackpot! Unfortunately, she refused to let my new friend in.

I was stuck.

All I could think of doing in my inebriated state was apologize to him—in my very broken high school French—and bid him adieu.

The next morning, I received an alarming phone call. Frenchie's fellow travelers were on the line, asking if I had any idea what happened to their friend. Once again, I reverted to my very best high school French and attempted to communicate that I had no idea.

Apparently, Frenchie had left not only his cell phone, cash, and ID back at his hotel room, but any and all remnants of who he was. After his friends tried searching for him all day (the only clue being that he had disappeared with some American chick), they finally filed a missing person's report with the Boston police.

Fortunately, Frenchie's friends eventually succeeded in tracking him down, but I was sick to my stomach for days for having kicked poor Frenchie to the curb—in a foreign country, no less!

I actually did see Frenchie again when he and his friends arrived in NYC. There, I learned that the guys were all massage therapists. Apparently, my curb-kicking was forgiven, as they generously offered me a free session, along with drugs, at their hotel in Brooklyn.

I graciously declined.

Leo Jr.

How is a girl supposed to cope with yet another bachelorette party, celebrating yet another friend finding love and leaving the hell that is the dating pool behind? Especially when that girl is on the cusp of ending a relationship with someone she dared hope might be "The One"?

For me, the occasion calls for only one thing: a vigorous round of making out with a total stranger whom I will never see again.

The lucky guy was a random twenty-five-year-old Leonardo Di Caprio look-alike. Of course, he did not hold an American passport—he was on holiday from Switzerland, where he was getting his master's degree. In what, I don't remember, but let me tell you, if they gave advanced degrees for lip locking, Little Leo would be on his way to a PhD! It was just the sugar I needed after all the stress of trying to figure out where yet another relationship was going.

Who needs relationships when you have Lip Sluthood?

What I've learned from being a Lip Slut:

- There's nothing like a good, old-fashioned make-out session to relieve stress, exercise your face, burn a couple of extra calories, and, most importantly, get a good case of the tingles—without having to wake up in someone else's bed the next day.

- Being a lip slut means not having to worry about what you look like naked.

Twelve

Mama's Boys

There's nothing quite as touching as the love between a mother and her son.

Unless, of course, you happen to be dating that son.

Then that powerful mother-son bond can suddenly turn a little creepy. Your man, who you assume should have eyes for you and only you, is actually equally (and quite possibly more) committed to another woman. And suddenly, you're plunged into a death match for the heart and soul of a person *she gave birth to.*

Ewwww.

It's not a fair fight. And, from my personal experience, it's a fight you want to avoid at all costs. Read on for the gory details.

Slot Machine

Picture a young, innocent Mary, fresh out of the gate after her painful divorce from Burak, ready to get back in the dating ring once again. I was so sweet. So vulnerable. That is why the guy I've come to call Slot Machine has continued to rank as one of the All-Time Worst of the Nicknames, even after all these years of Dating Hell.

Not that I knew this from the get-go. Slot Machine and I met on the dating site Plenty of Fish—long before I realized those were toxic waters. We even made it to the five-month mark, which, although I had no idea at the time, would be a true rarity in my "drive through" boyfriend history. I use the word "boyfriend" very generously.

I'm going to call Slot Machine "SM" from now on, because this is a long story and Slot Machine takes a lot longer to type! SM had a serious case of separation anxiety. He had finally moved out of his Mommy's house to take a job in the wilds of Connecticut. He still made the round-trip, four-hour drive every weekend to catch up with Mother, however.

Red flag!

Unfortunately, being a relative dating novice at this point, I completely overlooked the substantial significance of his weekly journey.

String issues aside, I must admit that the first couple of months were fantastic. He sent flowers to my office, which made me the talk of the town (or at least the seniors I worked with). I recruited him to run with me as I trained for my second marathon. Okay, he could barely keep pace with me, but it was nice to have the company. It was nice that he cared.

The day I noticed he had changed his Facebook status to "in a relationship," I felt a tingling all the way down to my toes. This was the first "relationship" since my ex. I was so excited!

Have you ever heard the saying, "be careful what you wish for"?

Because SM loved to play the slots, we decided to have some fun and take a trip together—our first—to Vegas (nickname alert!). He took care of all of the details and even arranged a suite for us at The Venetian. It was very exciting. Except this one little detail…

Why on Earth did he book our round-trip flights to Vegas out of Delaware?

Turns out he wanted me to meet his beloved Mother, as well as the rest of the family. To be honest, I was honored.

Like any good guest (that wasn't raised by wolves), I baked my famous chocolate chip cookies, bought a nice bottle of wine, and even borrowed my friend Fiona's favorite summer dress. I was, ready, willing, and actually quite anxious to meet his "awesome" relatives.

After what seemed like several days on the road, we pulled up to his house in some random suburban Delaware neighborhood. His family was in the midst of having a barbecue. Awesome! I love barbecues! It's so nice to escape the city on a hot summer afternoon for some greenery, good food, and scintillating conversation.

Unfortunately, number three was not an option.

SM's family from Nepal was also visiting—and I swear, they were like an Eastern Hemisphere version of the Honey Boo Boo family. The most memorable was SM's cousin, who had married a beautiful Nepalese woman and brought her to the barbeque to meet the family. For the life of me, I couldn't figure out what her home life must have been like to drive her into the hairy arms of this beast. 'Cuz was a big-boned dude, drunk out of his mind, and walked around the party with his hands down his pants. Yes, I know—a charmer. The other uncle, aunts, and cousins in attendance weren't much better.

But back to Cousin One. The day before I arrived, he had resurrected his homeland's custom of sacrificing a goat; right there in the back yard where we were eating. Apparently, goats and other animals are ritually slaughtered and eaten during the Hindu festival of Dashain. SM's family even insisted on showing me pictures of the barbaric event, which was not a lot of fun seeing as I'm an ardent animal lover.

Thank God they didn't wait for my arrival to perform their ancient ritual. I probably would have thrown up.

However, they were thoughtful enough to bring out the poor goat's horns and insist that I smell them, including the left over brain parts still inside. I wanted to be polite—I didn't want to be the Ugly American who looked down on their custom—but I just couldn't. When I declined, word immediately circulated that I was a stuck-up NYC bitch.

Suddenly, I was the butt of all their jokes. They insisted on pouring my beer—mine alone—into a glass. I tried to explain that I was perfectly happy drinking it out of the bottle, but they wouldn't hear of it.

Meanwhile, SM, apparently in his excitement to hug and kiss Mommy, left my cookies in the sweltering car, along with the wine. His mother finally insisted he retrieve them, but thanks to the heat they had reverted to batter. The litter of kids who spent the day jumping all over me devoured them (probably with spoons) in about ten seconds. No one drank the wine, so his mother kept trying to pawn it off on me.

I honestly don't think they knew how to open anything that doesn't come with a screw-off cap.

Then there was the aunt who made Honey Boo Boo's mother look like Princess Grace. When she found out I was from New York City, her only question for me was how many hot dog vendors there were on every street.

Sadly, I hadn't bothered to count before I left. Who knew how important this information would be for making a good impression?

As the evening progressed, the boys (who I believe are never to be men) came up with the genius idea of smashing a watermelon over one of their brainless heads and video-taping it. I happened to be sitting squarely in the blast zone; meaning Fiona's favorite dress was instantly splattered with bright pink goo.

I instantly yelled, "Shit!"

At this point, SM joined in the family chorus that yes, indeed, I was one stuck-up bitch.

When the Evening from Hell finally ended after what seemed like an eternity, I slept on the couch alone. The next morning, I awoke to a glorious surprise. Right next to me sat SM's gorilla of a cousin with his hand down his pants, holding a beer and snoring like some zoo animal.

All I could think was that I would have preferred the goat. They should have sacrificed this hog instead!

An hour later, the hoard of kids woke up and start-ed jumping on me all over again. Time to get the hell out of Dodge. We said our goodbyes and Mommy Dearest dropped us at an airport just outside the Delaware state line.

We were finally on our way to Vegas, albeit with a few stops along the way.

Do you know where the first stop was?

NEWARK! Yes, one of the three NYC airports. When I learned our destination was a mere cab ride from my apart-ment, my opinion of my boyfriend-of-five-months sank right down through the floor. I asked him why in the name of God he booked a flight out of Delaware when it originated where we actually lived?

Silence.

I was also speechless by the time the plane landed in New Jersey. I could only look out the window and stare at the New York skyline.

But, he did book the trip, and we were going to Vegas, and we were staying in the Venetian. So I held out some hope and said no more.

As we headed toward Vegas, I asked SM if I could listen to some music on his iPhone. This was almost six years ago, when the iPhone had just been launched. I had never used one before and was curious to see how it worked. He handed it over, and as I was trying to enter my contact information, I couldn't help noticing an email from Craigslist.

The subject? "How much are your services?"

I didn't mean to snoop; I was just trying to add my deets to his contact list, so I gave him the benefit of the doubt. After all, "services" could mean anything: painting services, handyman services, taxi services, anything.

Except, the next subject line happened to read, "Swingers in Delaware Newsletter."

Yikes. No wonder he was so attached to his home state!

I had to say something. We'd been together five months and I had no idea about this "interest" of his. I didn't want to cause a commotion in the middle of a plane-load of people, so I typed up what I had discovered and passed it to him.

Instantly, he became a person I had never seen before.

He was pissed off. He was defensive. He couldn't believe I had been sniffing around in his emails!

Come on, it was an accident! Besides, I think any girlfriend with half a brain would have reacted in the exact same way.

With the last of the celebratory, pre-Vegas mood broken, we spent the next couple of hours in stony silence. As soon as we disembarked, I ran to the bathroom to call Fiona—I needed advice, and hers is always great. I was contemplating just buying a ticket and flying home then and there.

But I didn't. Unfortunately.

We finally got to the hotel, exhausted from a twelve-hour flight that should have taken six hours, but SM wasn't too tired to start in on me again. The look of rage on his face and the tone of his voice actually scared me. At that point, we were thirty minutes late for the Cirque de Soleil show, so we trudged off in utter silence. I decided to keep my mouth shut and avoid any further discussion of The Topic, and we agreed to just have a good time.

After all, we were in Vegas—fun city!

Very fortunately, two of my sorority sisters were in town at the same time, so we met up with them. This lightened the mood substantially. We ended up at the Playboy Club, and then moved to a bar downstairs by the casino. At this point, SM excused himself to go to the bathroom.

He never came back.

I was getting nervous. I knew he was a little tipsy, but not drunk enough to just disappear. My thoughts started racing. Was he jumped in the john and left for dead? Did he suddenly join the Merchant Marines?

I called and texted at least a hundred times, but got no

response. My friend Molly and I searched every nook and cranny of all of the bathrooms (yes, including men's rooms) in the casino, but no luck. He had vanished without a trace.

Maybe he found a goat to sacrifice and got charged and gored?

It was anybody's guess.

By this point, maybe because of the stress, I was more than a little tipsy myself. Molly and I took a cab, but to the wrong hotel. I vaguely remember trying to give a poker dealer my room card. Not a good night all around. Finally, we made our way to the Venetian—luckily, Molly stuck with me; I couldn't even remember my room number. In fact, the front desk had to have security escort me to the right quarters.

When I opened the door, I was greeted by SM's bare, drunken ass waving in the air like a tattered flag on the Fourth of July.

I was too drunk to deal with another confrontation and passed out instead. I mustered up the courage to query him the next day as to why in hell he left me on the opposite end of the Strip when he said he was just going to the loo.

He claimed he had puked all over himself and was too embarrassed to return to the table, so he just up and left.

But... We were in Vegas. I really wanted to have fun, so we rallied and went for a couples' massage. It was a much needed tension reliever. Unfortunately, it was also short-lived. SM moved on to the whirlpool, where he claimed a hairy man sat next to him and waved his paw over his crotch. When he progressed to the steam room, his furry new friend, not one to be deterred, asked my true love if he wanted a blowjob! SM claimed he declined these advances, but that email about the Swingers in Delaware gave me a momentary pause as to which way he was actually swinging.

I spent the final two days of our fun-filled getaway alone at the pool, as SM claimed to be too hungover to get out of bed again until our departure day. Although, ever the romantic, I had brought a bottle of Dom Perignon along for our special vacation—which he didn't seem to have a problem slurping down.

The trip home was endless. What should have been a simple, five-hour flight lasted an unbelievable twenty-one hours! I could have landed in China or Australia sooner. We had to change planes twice, once in Colorado and again in D.C. When I dared to question him on our convoluted travel arrangements, he again called me a bunch of horrible names and got that same scary look in his eyes he had in our hotel room.

I just stayed quiet.

Our final stopping point? Delaware, of course! After all this, I was facing another day at the funny farm, followed by a four-hour car ride back to NYC.

Just kill me now.

At this point, SM let loose with an obscenity-laden barrage of insults that would have made a pirate blush. He said I never cared about him, and reminded me that his mother thought I was no-good and (again for the third time) one stuck up bitch. Of course, that made it true.

At that point, I had had enough. All I could think to say in response was, "You must have mistaken me for someone who gives a shit."

It didn't end with the trip. He continued to harass me

with the most hateful emails and texts for what seemed like months until, finally, one day, they stopped. Of course, the cherry on the sundae of our time together was his final message to "mail back my GPS if you haven't already smashed it in anger."

So I did (because I'm such a nice person), right to Mommy's front door.

Oh, and in case you haven't figured this out on your own—we broke up.

The Shabbat of Poo

I was enjoying a lovely Sunday brunch with my friends when I met The Shabbat of Poo, a nice, clean cut, good-looking, "every Jewish mother's son" type of guy. He was a native of the Upper East Side, a few years younger than me (28 to my 31 years), and adorable enough that I decided to rob the cradle and give him a shot.

Now, at this point in my dating life (recent, as opposed to ancient, history), I entered this potential liaison with my eyes wide open. There's no denying I left the restaurant with that tingly feeling brought on by the first blush of attraction. However, one of my girlfriends immediately warned me that most Jewish boys are taught, virtually from birth, that only a girl of the same religion will pass muster when it came time to meet Mother. Being the hopeless romantic I am, I decided to accept his invitation for dinner the following Sunday anyway.

I know, I know. I'm hopeless!

At that point, my hopes were running high. I was confident that if Mother ended up having any issues with my lack of Jewish-ness, I would prove her wrong. After all, I rationalized, why would he waste his time—and mine—if only a fellow Jew would do?

Poo was considerate enough to choose a restaurant in the little slice of heaven I call home—Hell's Kitchen—which was an indicator of the way the dinner would turn out. There, I learned that Poo was an only child who rarely brought a girl home to meet his parents.

Especially his mother.

Before the entrée even arrived, it was crystal clear that not only was his mother a complete control freak, but as a result, she had produced the consummate Mama's Boy. Score: Mommy, 10 – Mary, 0! But I wanted to know more, so I proceeded to the million-dollar question. Were the rumors actually true? Was a Nice Jewish Girl really the only acceptable candidate for a mate?

When confirmation of my worst fears exploded from his mouth at the speed of a just-launched rocket, two thoughts instantly and almost simultaneously popped into my head:

1. Why he would waste his time and mine?

2. Oh, like most men, he probably just wants to get laid.

What better target for a hook-up than a lowly *shiksa*, who, like a paper towel, one could use as needed and throw away? Well, score one for Team *Shiksa*. I stood firm that this turn of events just wasn't going to happen on my watch.

However, it gets better, because the evening ended with a decidedly unplanned, but eerily perfect, retribution. After he walked me back to my apartment (like the Nice

Jewish Boy he is), Poo asked if he could come up to use the bathroom.

I coolly and a bit flirtatiously flipped my hair back, kind of like Beyonce on tour. I attempted to insert a bit of levity into what had been an otherwise "meh" night by jokingly saying, "I hope I flushed the toilet!"

He scurried off to take care of business. Upon exiting the lavatory, he was stiff and quiet, with the weirdest expression I've ever seen planted on his face. I turned at least a hundred different shades of red as I realized that my little attempt at levity was actually no laughing matter.

Whoopsie!

But, hey, give me a break, I live alone. I'm a bachelorette. These things happen!

Of course, that's with the benefit of hindsight. At the time, I was mortified. I apologized at least a million times and did everything short of washing his shoes with my hair to make up for the faux pas. I finally had to practically kick his knees in the back to loosen him up enough to sit down on my couch.

Then, at the exact moment he was barely able to cough out, "Don't worry about it," my precious little dog, perhaps sensing mommy's queasy and uneasy feelings over a night full of rejection and humiliation, jumped up and peed on poor Poo's lap!

What's a mother to do?

In my case, my inner Lip Slut sprung to desperate life, and all I could think to do was to shove my tongue down Poo's throat to somehow distract his (and my) thoughts away from my toilet and my dog pee and the general restroom-centric theme of our evening.

Unfortunately, it didn't help. I felt so completely uncomfortable that I told him we should call it a night. He vacated my apartment at the speed of the Tasmanian devil.

Of course, I never heard from Poo again, but the night wasn't a total loss. I'll bet he thinks twice before going out with another *goy*.

Score one for the team!

What Mama's Boys have taught me:

- You will always be second, so become best friends with his mother. If you can't, get really good at pretending.

- According to my friend Rose, who is dating an MB, you will have to win him over through his stomach. Become a better cook than his mother.

- Never make him choose. If you're in a serious relationship, become a part of the family so there isn't division. If it is super serious, bring both families together. Unless they make a habit of sacrificing animals in the backyard.

Thirteen
Assessing the Prospects

So, we're thirteen chapters into this book and, as you've probably gathered, I've been on a lot of dates. Not just a lot of dates, but a lot of terrible, horrible, no good, very bad dates (to paraphrase a beloved children's book—it just seems to fit the situation).

The question is, what have I learned from my experiences when it comes to determining if a date will turn out to be a keeper or wind up on the ever-growing scrap-heap of Dating Disasters?

I've learned how to assess the prospects. I'm about to teach you to do the same.

You might want to take some notes.

Here are my Ten Tips for Assessing a Prospect.

PHASE ONE: BEFORE YOU SAY YES
ATP Tip #1 – Fish in the Right Waters

Your first exposure to a prospect is likely going to be his profile picture, provided you're fishing online (more on that later). How do you judge a photo that has been carefully chosen to present the best possible image of a prospect (or, at least, what he thinks is the best possible image)? Here are a few tips.

First—and this is a warning for women who live anywhere, not just in Manhattan—if a guy's profile shot is of him in the bathroom taking a photo with his cell phone, and if, in this picture, his abs are the focal point, DO NOT TALK TO HIM. This reeks of Jersey Shore and we are mature ladies. No need to get into a Situation.

As a New York girl, this is why I now limit my dating to my neighbors on the Isle of Manhattan, and occasionally allow a prospect from Brooklyn to slip through. I've found these men to actually act like men. (Well…not all of them. But most of them when compared to the guys from the outer boroughs!) They usually post normal pictures of themselves, either in a business suit, or on vacation somewhere, or just out having a good time.

That's what nearly always separates the men from the "borough boys."

For example, if a guy's from Brooklyn, nine times out of ten he'll post an artistic, hipster-esque profile picture. Often in black and white, just to amp up the artistry factor.

How can you tell if a prospect hails from Queens or Staten Island? Those borough boys are obsessed with their muscles, and therefore tend to have pictures of their abs or other pumped-up body parts in their profile pictures.

Prospects from the Bronx think toughness is the true measure of a man. So expect photos highlighting their tattoos. If you have a weakness for bad boys, be warned!

Of course, I'm generalizing here. Nevertheless, if you're dipping your toe in the New York City dating pool, my advice is to stick with prospects that live in Manhattan or Brooklyn. Of course, this can be a tough call, especially in the treacherous waters of the online dating world. However, as there will of course be some communication (pictures, emails, phone calls, etc.) between the two of you before you actually take the plunge of meeting in person, I urge you to perform your due diligence.

More on that topic later.

Remember, there are other ponds to fish in besides online dating sites. In fact, if you're "married" to that vehicle, may I politely suggest a trial separation?

To which, you might reply, "Where else am I going to meet men?"

I'm so glad you asked!

One of the best ways to put yourself in a better position to find that special someone is to join groups, go to meetings, hang out at events, etc., that you have a genuine interest in. This puts you in close proximity to prospects that already like the same things you do—for real!

These situations not only give you "face time" with those prospects, but an opportunity to learn a new thing or two in the process. A friend of mine took up marathon running and, in the process, not only lost twenty pounds and got into the best shape of her life, but also met an absolutely terrific guy! I haven't given up hope; I'm on my third marathon and eighth half-marathon and I still haven't run into the man of my dreams, but the point is, never give up! Smile and carry on.

Dating can be very frustrating. My girl Amber dated a guy for six years, and after they broke up she was sure she would never be ready to date ever again. Four months later, she met the guy she will most likely spend the rest of her life with. I'm not sure if it was a case of being in the right place at the right time or if it was destiny, but I call them the Hurricane Sandy couple. They met at a bar after the electricity was turned back on in the East Village, and the rest is history.

ATP Tip #2 – Talk is Not Cheap!

This is where that whole due diligence thing comes into play.

It's no joke—this is important. Sizing up potential dates should be viewed as something like interviewing a potential roommate. That's why part of my assessment process is asking any potential date to give me a ring (yes, I mean on the phone) before we meet. Those quick chats can be invaluable in determining if there's a sign a guy isn't the right fit—or that he's completely crazy. After all, I don't want to waste my time, and neither should you.

I find that sometimes guys are surprised when you ask them to call you before a date because *nobody* calls on the phone anymore; everybody texts. However, I've been told by prospective suitors that they actually like it when a girl asks them to give her a quick ring before a date.

Of course, he gets bonus points if he calls without you having to suggest it!

As for the due diligence part, a call will help you assess the following:

- You can get a sense of whether or not there's any hint of crazy in his voice

- You can assure yourself that chances are slim the prospect will chop you up into itty bitty pieces and throw you into the East River (see Crazy Eyes in Chapter 5)

- You can confirm the prospect is familiar with the English language (see Turkish Rose in Chapter 9)

- You can predict whether or not conversation will flow when you actually meet in real life

- You can get an idea of whether or not the prospect will be fun to hang out with, so you'll be looking forward to the date even more—and may even get to access your Lip Slut (Chapter 11)

You get the idea.

Another reason the quick phone chat is so important is that you can actually use your landline—the one you forgot you had, that you got when you had to buy the three-in-one bundled Time Warner package for the discounted rate. Of course, you'll need to remember your phone number to do it. My landline number is stored in my cell phone. Using a landline phone is so retro cool.

ATP Tip #3 – Examine that Email!

Another important occasion for due diligence is when you get an email from a potential date. That email is more than just communication. It's a great place to scout for red flags before your date even starts. Emails are the best way, short of hiring a private eye, to (discretely) ascertain when a prospect's last relationship was—and how it ended. You don't want any ex-wives or girlfriends stalking you or peeking in the windows, especially if you live on the first floor.

Yes, this has actually happened—to me.

I've also discovered that a lot of guys tend to sign up on dating sites just a couple of months after breaking up with girlfriends of three plus years. I don't want to be anyone's rebound, and neither do you, so do your research!

As an example of what you can learn from emails, here are two actual emails I recently received.

Prospect: How is it you're single I will never fully comprehend. You're in New York... I'm in New York... This online dating business is so bourgeois.

Wait for it...* clears throat*... Alrighty then, when are we grabbing drinks? :)

Seconds after I checked out his profile, I got another email. I assume he must have gotten a message that I viewed his profile, which he took as an invitation to not give me time to reply to his first email before he sent a second. Weird!

Prospect: Ok ok... I know, I tend be rather verbose in this time honored tradition of wooing a woman. It's an arduous process to undertake, and not for the faint of heart.

What can I say, I aim to satiate. Here at HoweMade Inc, quality service is something we strive for. Ingenuity, sophistication, and elegance together in one classy bottle, served with panache, savoir-faire and smothered in Ghirardelli-flavored tiger blood.

What's your number? Ahhhhhh I can smell the dollar pizza slices and PBR already! Philandering and cuddling optional, yet highly recommended.

Besos.

Did he say actually say *tiger blood?* Is Charlie Sheen trying to ask me out?

Of course, you can also do some due diligence without even getting an email. That's what Facebook, LinkedIn, and Google are for. Remember, it's not considered stalking if it's research! Don't deny it, we have all googled someone's name at least once in our lives.

PHASE TWO: THE FIRST MEETING
ATP Tip #4 – Have a Positive Attitude

Try not to be too judgmental when you first meet your prospect in person. Of course, if he's simultaneously picking his nose and scratching his ass, and/or constantly adjusting his balls, move along.

I've always tried to approach a date with a new guy with a fresh, positive outlook (call me "Little Miss Sunshine") and make every possible effort to NOT let past dating disasters interfere with the man of the moment. Remember, there is no universal truth when it comes to individuals. We all have our own strengths and weaknesses—we are all like unique little snowflakes. The trick is to try to find a guy whose personality complements yours, and vice versa.

ATP Tip #5 – Keep it Casual

I believe that when you're first meeting a prospect, casual is best. I advocate a venue with an easy exit—like a back door—in case you realize a mistake has been made early on.

Because of this, many women I know choose Starbucks as their regular go-to place for a first meeting. Personally, I prefer getting together for a cocktail. Caffeine makes you nervous; alcohol helps you relax. Of course, that doesn't mean I'm advising you to get *too* relaxed. Limit your cocktail intake—after all, as the old saying goes, "One martini, two martini, three martini, floor!" Is that extra buzz really worth the very real possibility of waking up next to a mutant the next morning, or nursing a bad hangover the next day at work? Survey says… ABSOLUTELY NOT!

ATP Tip #6: Be Aware of His Cell Phone

An early red flag for potential disaster is your date's cell phone. No, not whether he's an iPhone or an Android man, or even if his phone weighs over a pound and was first acquired in the '90s. Or if it's a flip phone—which I find many blue collar guys still have.

I'm talking about how much action the phone in question gets.

For example, if your date constantly checks his cell phone, or leaves it on the table so he can glance at it for any incoming messages, this is not a good sign. If he answers his phone or texts during a first date, that's even worse. Any of these phone-related faux pas should be taken as a warning sign of what's to come (like possibly being ignored and neglected and treated like second fiddle to his phone if you were to get into a relationship with this person).

I know this from experience. Remember Burak, my ex-husband? Once his business took off, he paid more attention to his phone than he did to me. I have also been on my share of first dates where I felt almost as neglected as I did when I was trapped in a loveless marriage. It is like the phone is the prospect's girlfriend, and you're the babe on the side he's having an affair with.

I don't care if a prospect runs his own business—in fact,

if he does run his own business, it's even more important that a guy is able to separate work from play. So these days, first dates with the phone-obsessed don't turn into second dates.

PHASE THREE: THE SECOND DATE
ATP Tip #7 – A Sniff is Worth a Thousand Words

Does your date pass the smell test? Believe it or not, the fact that a prospect chooses the right cologne (and the right amount to use) can be a very good sign that he's a keeper.

Why?

Because it shows he took that extra step to show he cares—even if the entire date winds up smelling like yesterday's garbage by the time it's over.

ATP Tip #8 – Is Your Dinner a Winner?

If your prospect makes reservations at an expensive, fancy restaurant, you might think you're in for an enchanted evening.

Maybe. Then again, maybe not.

Prospects have been known to take a girl to a Michelin star eatery, only to split a couple of appetizers and skip the entrees entirely.

If that's the case, trust me, it's time to run! This has happened to me a few times, and honestly, I would have been happier going to Olive Garden or Red Lobster and enjoy a full meal and some real conversation. There's nothing worse than a poser!

ATP Tip #9 – Ditch the Disappearing Act

After reading about my adventures in this department, this should really go without saying. But sometimes, you don't know your prospect is actually no longer a prospect and has already disappeared on you.

How can you tell? You go on one or two dates. The chemistry is amazing, the kiss is beyond wonderful, and the conversation is awesome. If that's not enough, he texts you something along the lines of, "You are different from the other girls and I can't wait until we meet again."

Then you never hear from him again. No text, no call, no email.

I know it doesn't seem fair, but there's a reason why it happens—and the reason is not you, it's him. Guys seem to lack that filter that says, "Maybe you shouldn't say that." As a species, they seem to think it's perfectly fine to say whatever's on their mind in the moment. Even if, an hour later, they feel completely differently, which they very well might.

That doesn't mean you should keep your guard up at all times (although this has definitely been an issue for me, especially as the dates have piled up). It just means that it's okay to move on without looking back. There's no point in replaying that last date in your mind over and over again, or trying to figure out if you said or did something wrong. Some things simply can't be explained. Men, unfortunately, can be one of them.

ATP Tip #10 – Put on your Poker Face

Why? Well, dating is a lot like poker: Everyone has their "tells." Some of those tells can be potential red flags. They include:

- What was your first reaction when you saw him in person? Did you want to jump his bones right there, or discreetly vomit into a nearby trashcan?

- Is he focused on your baby blues (or greens, or browns, or hazels) when you talk, or is he looking around the room, particularly at other women (like Rico Suave in Chapter 4)? If so, it's a pretty good indication that he is A) not interested in you, B) he is a womanizer, or C) all of the above! Drop him. It will only get worse—and you deserve better.

- Does the man have manners? If you are eating together, does he use the proper utensils or dine as though he was raised by wolves? Does he talk with his mouth full like a cow chewing its cud? Does he use his sleeve to wipe his mouth? Most importantly, is he someone you'd proudly invite to "break bread" with your closest friends, or even your parents? Maybe it sounds like I'm exaggerating here, but these little details are important. Remember, he's probably at his best in the early phase of dating. If things are already bad, chances are they won't improve during the course of your relationship.

- Does he have a sense of humor? If your answer is yes, is it at your expense? (Run!) The ability to find the funny is a great quality and makes conversation so much easier—especially when it includes some measure of self-deprecation. Sharing life with a funny guy makes its burdens much easier to bear.

- Is he relaxed? Is he nervous? Those first dates can naturally be nerve-wracking for any guy (or you!) and some very worthwhile candidates might benefit from a first-date Xanax. However, if you have to swat him off the ceiling to continue a conversation, or if he feels compelled to count everything in eights, it's probably best to call it a day.

- What does he talk about? As the old saying goes, "All work and no play make Jack a dull boy." Beware of the "Jacks" of this world. If his conversation consists of an endless monologue about his job (especially if that job is, say, as an investment banker or corporate exec), you might get sick of it fast, no matter how much you want him to be The One. Plus, it's beyond annoying to listen to a load of self-serving bullshit. I don't care how much money he makes, or how much you might fantasize about jet setting around the world with him and drinking champagne (or, in my case, martinis)—if you still can't shake the nagging twinge in your belly, move on. On the other hand, if his conversation shows he is genuinely interested in you, chances are (provided he's not a Disappearing Act), there are more dates in your future.

- Does he talk about sex too much? How much is too much? Well, if it makes you uncomfortable, that's a sign that he needs to tone down the NC-17 crap! Men are famous for thinking with their "little heads," so while a couple of off-color jokes may be fine with you, if he starts getting too specific (as in, "Do you have your own dom attire or should I just rent some at the dungeon?") I'd whip my ass out of there faster than you can say, "I'll take mine to GO!" (See Gelato in Chapter 9). Also, if he sends you any dick pics, RUN!

- If he doesn't call or text, isn't enthusiastic about seeing you, cancels your first date (which recently happened to one of my girlfriends) and doesn't try to set up a second or third date, avoids you like the plague when you're trying to introduce him to your friends or doesn't want to introduce you to his—MOVE ON!

- Not to sound shallow, but a prospect should have a job: You don't want to end up having to pay for everything. Also, pay attention to his living situation, educational background, hobbies, style of dress, who he's friends with, and what kind of conversations you have with him. He should smell good, have confidence, and last, but not least, must be able to handle YOUR personality.

Bottom line, if you're going to date a prospect, he should make you laugh, turn you on, and be sweet and dependable.

I promise, it's not too much to ask.

The fact is, the vast, vast majority of your dates are not going to develop into lasting relationships. Dating just doesn't work that way.

If it did, I would have been married at least thirty-seven times.

So, while I fully advocate welcoming each new prospect with an open mind, and even an open heart, you should accompany those very friendly body parts with open eyes and ears.

And yes, in case you're wondering, open legs are a no-no.

Use your gut instinct. It will never steer you wrong.

Fourteen
Appearance Counts

In the last chapter, I mentioned "style of dress" as something you might want to consider when deciding whether a prospect scores a second date with you. This is a topic that I believe deserves further exploration. Two of my favorite dating disasters happen to fall into the category I call "Appearance Counts."

The thing is, there are plenty of different "styles" of dress: professional, fashion-forward, preppy, casual, sporty... You get the idea. But there are also plenty of guys out there to whom the word "style" doesn't exactly apply—unless it follows the phrase "lack of." Read on, and you'll see what I mean.

Ecko Red

Remember when I said I try not to date guys who inhabit locales outside the Isle of Manhattan? The guy I like to call Ecko Red is one good reason why. Somehow, this resident of the Bronx by way of Bulgaria (go figure!) actually made it over the first hurdle in the online dating game, and we agreed to meet.

Big mistake.

Now, I didn't presume he would show up looking like George Clooney at the Oscars, but my expectations regarding how a man should present himself (particularly on a first date) are pretty standard.

And this guy was certainly not what I expected.

When I met him at a lounge uptown—for our date—there stood a guy in a fire engine red Ecko fleece, with a crappy, worn out tee shirt underneath.

Seriously! Do first impressions count for nothing anymore?

There's nothing like an Ecko fleece to instantly turn me off. It takes me back to high school on Long Island, when we were all passing around a blunt in someone's parents' basement. Maybe Ecko is the official uniform of the outer boroughs?

So when my date showed up not only sporting Ecko, but the brightest, loudest, most obvious piece of clothing in the Ecko repertoire, I couldn't help thinking, "Is this the best you can come up with? For the love of God, don't you own at least one shirt with buttons on it? Did all of the Gaps burn down?"

Sadly, the fact that ER dressed like a seventeen-year-old and was in his thirties was only the tip of the iceberg of wrongness I was about to experience. He worked in the airline industry, so he must have made okay money to buy some decent clothes. He should have just donned a pilot suit. Maybe it would have conjured up images of Tom Cruise in Top Gun and I wouldn't have been so caught up in all that red.

Because not only did ER dress loud, he *was* loud. The

guy just would not stop talking about himself and what an awesome, awesome guy he was, and how he always treats his women with the utmost respect, "like gold."

Where was the respect for me?

The whole, almost entirely one-sided, conversation made me a little nauseated. Besides, how do you treat somebody like gold, anyway? Was he planning to smelt me into a brick?

When the bill came, Mr. Respectful oh-so-gallantly declared, "It's a first date, so I'll get this." I know he meant well and was trying to impress me with that golden touch of his, but seriously, sometimes a guy should just keep his mouth shut. Of course, I still offered to pay my half.

Because that's the kind of girl I am. Should I say I treat my dates "like gold?"

After he picked up the tab, ER was respectful enough to give me a ride home—even though it made him late to pick up a friend at the airport. That really was very gentlemanly. Especially for a guy wearing a bright red fleece.

Honestly, he did seem like a nice guy. Maybe he acted a little crazy because he was nervous. Maybe he was robbed recently and all his decent clothes were stolen, and he was left with nothing more than a fleece from his high school days and a grungy tee shirt. Hey, shit happens.

Because I didn't get past the blinding Ecko Red to check out his shoes (which could be the ultimate deal-breaker), I agreed to go out on a second date with him. Although I did make a mental note: If he showed up wearing Fila or Nike AIR, it would definitely be game over!

Unfortunately, once I agreed to go on a second date

with ER, I was hit with a non-stop barrage of texts. It practically took an act of Congress to get him to stop.

That second date? Never happened.

It's Not Easy Being Green

Some of my most memorable encounters with the opposite sex have happened on what I have now personally come to believe is one of the grossest days of the year in NYC. I'm talking about St. Patrick's Day, the annual no holds barred, drink till you piss on the street and pass out in it celebration of total debauchery. When all the underage guidos from Long Island, Westchester and North Jersey wear green and get smashed. No offense to the Irish, I love a good celebration, but after the experiences you will read below you will understand why I now lock myself inside my apartment with my dog Val until the day is over. In fact, it is 10:51 a.m. on St. Paddy's day as I edit this book, and I can already hear the bridge and tunnel debauchery starting outside my window on 9th Avenue.

Shudder.

Every St Patrick's Day, the stars of the show are invariably New York's finest—yes, the same men in blue who are usually sworn to preserve and protect us. My advice? Don't get mugged on St. Patrick's Day, ever! Not only will the cops be too inebriated to help you, the sight of these men in uniform, beer in one hand and a revolver in the other, might make you want to leave work early and run for cover.

If you aren't already wasted yourself, that is.

Of course, as the consummate party girl, I'm not one to run and hide. Nope, I used to be right in the middle of the action, chugging down with the best of them. This was when

I was sowing my wild oats post-divorce. That can lead to some nasty surprises a few days down the line. I've learned my lesson.

For example, about a week after one particularly wild St. Paddy's Day, I received a phone call from a firefighter who said I had given him my number. I had no memory of this exchange whatsoever, but firefighters can be very sexy. I figured, what the hell? If I gave him my number, he must be cute, right? I agreed to meet him for lunch at the World Financial Center later that week.

That's when I discovered just how strong beer goggles can be.

When my firefighter and I met again, he appeared to still be in full St. Paddy's Day celebration mode. What else could explain the fact that he was an absolute blur of green—including his teeth, his skin, and even the drippings from his nose?

His unique color scheme also included yellow—he actually wore sandals, which exposed his nasty, yellow, hairy, disease-ridden toenails. Even his shirt was dirty.

No wonder I could barely eat a bite of my salad. There was too much throwing up in my mouth going on.

Of course, he called me again, and just couldn't understand why I didn't want a second chance to bask in the glory of his…colorful presence.

Needless to say, after that experience, my beer goggles are history!

What I've learned about men and their appearance:

- Two words: BEER GOGGLES! Leave them for the under-thirty set—you're too old (and too smart) for this shit.

- First impressions count. I'm still suffering red fleece flashbacks.

- The mere fact that a man fights fires does not automatically make him hot.

Fifteen
Mixed Nuts

No matter how carefully you assess your prospects, no matter how much Google stalking and email analyzing and phone interviewing you do, if you date as regularly and often as I do, one or two crazies are bound to slip through. It's just a reality of dating. Some guys are really, really good at hiding the fact that they may be a danger to themselves—and possibly others. And sometimes, we girls can be just as good at ignoring the obvious signs.

As I've said before, shit happens. Show me a girl with a nut-job-free dating record, and I'll show you a girl who hasn't been on a lot of dates.

On the other hand, a woman who's spent a few years in the dating pool probably has at least a few stories like these.

Karaoke Superstar

Every girl has a secret dream of dating a superstar. A karaoke superstar, not so much. Unfortunately, the guy I will now refer to as KS was as close as I've gotten to the limelight so far.

I met KS on OkCupid, which was kind of ironic, because he wasn't exactly OK. At least, not in a mental health sense. This was evident from the start, when, once we got past the usual niceties (I liked your profile, I think we have a lot in common) and exchanging cell phone numbers, he started maniacally texting me.

He even suggested that we immediately FaceTime on our iPhones—something I found to be more than a little strange, considering we'd never even met in person.

I declined the generous FaceTime invite, but did opt in for some major phone time: Almost two hours that first night! During our conversation, I learned KS was born and raised in Greenwich Village and he was one of eight from a litter of children his poor mother had probably birthed on the kitchen table.

But that's not the interesting part. KS also claimed he was a retired member of an elite detective squad, and in the course of duty, he had been shot numerous times.

Or, as he explained, his "luck ran out."

Of course I spent two hours on the phone with the guy! I was talking to a real-life American hero! Who had taken a bullet! Definitely not your run-of-the mill online dating encounter.

But something was still a little off.

Like when KS went on to explain that he was super intelligent and had graduated from high school at the age of 14, attended college at 15, and even went on to study at the prestigious Princeton University. Okay, that's believable, I guess.

But—and here's where it got weird—it turns out KS had many, many interests. He was also a dog trainer, a personal trainer, and he worked with disadvantaged children at a local school. I was surprised, at this point, that he hadn't slapped on a wig and tried out for Miss America.

However, his true calling and talent lay in—you guessed it—karaoke singing.

KS believed he was a true gift to the musical world, and found no greater satisfaction than belting out tunes at bars dedicated to great, undiscovered talents like him. He was so good at this, he explained, that one very special evening, he was actually approached by a Sony executive (undoubtedly drunk) at a bar in Brooklyn.

This big-time exec was so blown away by KS's singing talents, at least according to KS, that he flew the aspiring "star" out to California, where KS claims to have auditioned for the TV show *The Voice*.

Looking back, yes, it sounds more than a little crazy. However, at the time, I shamefully admit I was flattered. I actually kind of liked the fact that he texted me virtually non-stop for the next seventy-two hours. Or more.

Even though our exchange, as you will see, was hardly what I'd consider normal. Although, it didn't start out full-on crazy...

KS: *Just sent you me singing.*

ME: *Maybe I can see you perform one day!*

KS: *Of course! What's your schedule like?*

ME: *Days off are Sun. and Mon. But I guess normal hours.*

KS: *Maybe Saturday night?*

ME: I'm going to be partying in Brooklyn right after the half-marathon...day drinking! If I get a 2nd wind for Sat. evening I would love to meet up. Maybe Sunday would be better?

KS: Can try for Sunday, but that's my cooking day lol (yes I cook as well). Would you venture back into Brooklyn? I'm only like 15 mins on the 1 train.

ME: We will figure it out.

KS: Sounds good. I make a mean white sangria.

ME: I prefer white sangria – but I'm not going to your place on a first date!

KS: No way. That's why Sat. night would have been op-timal. I would go to your hood. My friend's bar is in your area and has karaoke. What are you up to tonight?

ME: No plans really. I'm still waiting for the handyman! Wanna do something later?

KS: Unfortunately I'm helping a friend that owns his own karaoke company. I helped him get a new Monday night gig and tonight's the first night.

ME: That's awesome!

KS: You have an iPhone?

ME: Yes sir!

KS: Cool. Maybe FaceTime later?

ME: I've never done that before!

KS: Lol. I do it with my parents every weekend.

The next day it got a tiny bit weird...

ME: Little nervous about this face time stuff! lol

KS: Why? That way at least we'll see each other before we meet and it won't feel that "awkward."

KS: Send me some more pics. Any bikini pics?

ME: Too much too soon

KS: I worked out last night. I did 2,000 crunches lol

ME: Yeah u can take the crunches

KS: Send me some more pics of yourself bella!

ME: A pic for a pic

KS: Me without a beard, baby faced lol! Home yet?

Sends pic

ME: Ya

KS: Send me a pic of yourself the way you look now.

ME: We will see each other soon enough!

KS: You're no fun. Sweet dreams bella. Text me tomorrow..

Then, the next day...

KS: *How's your day Bella?*

ME: *Not bad. Trying to make my grand escape.*

KS: *Wanna FaceTime tonight?*

He wants to FaceTime again?! Didn't I tell him no the first five times!

ME: *That sounds dirty...*

KS: *Well you did say you like it dirty. Oh okay. Hot date? lol*

ME: *Yes I have one this weekend ;)*

KS: *Let me know what they look like lol. And, be careful. I'll talk to you in an hour lol. Well good night. Hope you got home safe.*

ME: *Nighty night!*

KS: *Never heard back. We'll talk tomorrow. Sweet dreams bella.*

Never heard back? Weird comment.
    And the next day...

KS: *Hello there...miss me already? lol Are you going home to nap after your race?*

ME: *No, I'm going to have some cocktails with running*

buddies and ride the rides at Coney Island. :) Finally free!!!

Then, two hours later…

KS: *Helloooooooo??*

Then later, at almost 4:00 a.m. when I didn't reply back to his last text…

KS: *Not going.*

KS: *Decided not to meet you.*

ME: Why?

KS: *Cuz I don't trust you*

ME: Umm, this is weird.

KS: *Yeah you've been a bit disconnected doesn't feel right. So whoever you've met, well then have fun with him. Just don't want to be fake and act like anything is the same.*

ME: What r u talking about? R u serious? We've been texting non-stop all week! I was sleeping by 9:00 last night. I was looking forward to meeting u tomorrow. Wtf r u talking about?

KS: *I'm talking about the last 3 nights. We could have talked after work or whatever and you've decided not to. You've been out and about with "friends" and it's* *cool. Hope you've met the right guy, just appreciate honesty.*

ME: R u serious?! We spoke 2 hours Tues. and Wed. I went out with my girlfriends. Last night I passed out by 9:00. I can't even believe I'm explaining myself!! This is nuts!!!!

KS: *Then you should have been honest with me! You left work at 6:30 talked about your marathon and that was it?? The night before, out with your friend and that was it?? No contact with me.*

ME: I work a lot, I rarely go out during week, and I'm def. not gallivanting around town. I am so taken back by these messages and a little turned off by u! Because I thought we had great conversation the other night, I rearranged my schedule so we could meet tomorrow night cause I was looking forward to skipping this texting thing and meeting u. But now I'm turned off and in shock! And disappointed! We are adults! And you're acting like a teenager! I feel like I've wasted my time!

KS: *I wasn't trying to complicate things but at the same time you not returning texts was a bit daunting. If you can find it in your heart to forgive I'd still like to meet you.*

ME: Let's talk tonight I'll be home.

KS: *Please call me around 8:00 if you're home.*

ME: I will.

I never called.

KS: *Sorry about it all. What's up? On my way to sing. Hey, so wanna meet this weekend? Giant frozen drinks?*

ME: I would like to but I'm just nervous. Let's say we were dating and I went out with my girlfriend. You would freak out! That's the vibe I feel from u.

KS: *No, I wouldn't. I think you going out with your friends and hanging with mine is healthy. I'm just cautious. Remember what I did for 10 years. (Like getting shot 4 times as a detective in Detroit.) I've seen some bad things happen to good people and I'm just cautious of that. But, I'm not like what you portray me as.*

ME: Or think I was banging some guy? Totally the vibe; but I'm around this weekend, so I'm open to meeting.

KS: *I'm really not like that. Why don't we meet up on Saturday afternoon?*

ME: Cool. But I wanna spend a few hours after work with Valentino as I pick him up Saturday 5:30! So, probably the later the better Saturday. I'm gonna feel bad if I leave Valentino alone too long on his first day in the big city. :)

KS: *So let's FaceTime at 9:30? It'll be fun.*

Again with the FaceTime? Maybe he should buy stock in Apple!

ME: I'm really not feeling FaceTime tonight I feel gross. Can't wait for weekend.

KS: *Really want the weekend. Frozen drinks!!!! Lol*

The next day…

KS: *What are you up to?*

ME: At the beach. Gorgeous day!! We just got busted by beach patrol for having a beer! Ridiculous!

KS: *Should have told me you were going.*

ME: I'm with my girlfriend.

KS: *Are you home?*

ME: I won't be home 'til closer to 11:30.

KS: *Where you at?*

ME: At my girlfriend's.

KS: *What? lol the night before you were at your friends till 11:30pm lol*

ME: And?

KS: *Stating the obvious lol. You said you fall asleep early on school nights so that was an example how you didn't.*

ME: Do u want to meet Sunday?

KS: *Why Sunday? Busy this weekend?*

ME: *I don't really go out Fridays u know this.*

KS: *Never mind.*

After all that…I still went out with him!

I hadn't just hit bottom. I'd fallen right through the floor to find a whole other level of bottom!

I don't know why I went through with the date. Normally, I would have been turned off by such constant, unwarranted attention. But I really felt like we hit it off on the phone.

What can I say? Again, I'm a hopeless romantic.

I agreed to meet him in person at the "renowned" Dallas Barbecue (his idea, definitely not mine) downtown. There, we indulged in the aforementioned big, frozen drinks. Now, I'm not usually a fan of the sweet, frozen kind of alcohol unless I'm in the kind of tropical locale where beverages always come with a slice of pineapple and a paper umbrella.

However, on this occasion, I made an exception. I sucked back my giant drink in record time so that we could move on to a location where I wouldn't feel like I might get jumped.

That's when we "conveniently" stumbled upon KS's favorite karaoke spot. What were the odds?!

I couldn't help but wonder if KS had planned this particular detour from the beginning. We just *happened* to be in the neighborhood. Once we were settled, and I had followed up my big, frozen beverage with a more respectable martini, KS *happened* to take the stage—where he dedicated his first tune to yours truly.

Lucky me.

I don't claim to be a music critic or anything. I'm no expert. However, as I stared down toward the end of the bar where his big performance was taking place, I kept wondering whether I had had one too many, or if he really was just as bad as he sounded.

Let's just say KS was definitely not *The Voice* worthy.

The ballad seemed to go on forever. When it ended, I wished it *had* gone on forever, because now I had to tell him what I thought of the performance. Yikes.

I choked my olive down and, clearing my throat, told him he was "great."

Never were quotation marks more richly deserved.

Still, we somehow, at some point, ended up back at my apartment. Apparently, I had agreed to introduce him to my dog. After all, one of his many pursuits was an aspiring "dog whisperer." At some point, the lights went out. The night ended up blurring into morning and... I woke up with him still next to me.

I have to admit, the sleeping together part (and God only knows what that entailed) was, in fuzzy retrospect, more fun than the slushy, larger than my head, Saturday Night Fever karaoke.

But, now that I was fully conscious, the fun was over. My Superstar refused to take his act out of my apartment. He just wouldn't leave—even though I spent the entire day in exaggerated moaning and complaining about my hangover. Even when I pretended to be yakking in the bathroom, he just would not GO!

It was 5:00 p.m. when I finally succeeded in kicking him out.

I've never felt more relieved in my life.

But our relationship was still not over... Because he still had my phone number!

KS: *Guess you were busy.*

ME: *I'm playing with Valentino lol.*

KS: *All night? Didn't hear from you since 2pm*

ME: *Umm. I worked 'til 7:30 then went to happy hour*

KS: *Too bad. Could have been golden. Good luck with yourself.*

ME: *Excuse me?? Wtf r u talking about?*

KS: *You're not very consistent and you are very defensive. Would have been nice to spend more time with you but it seems like you don't want it. Good luck with your issues. I really enjoyed our time together.*

I thought about responding—and possibly suggesting therapy.

Then I thought about how a totally insane former detective who was clearly obsessed with me might react to a not-so-nice text.

Needless to say, I never found out if he made the cut on *The Voice*, because I just never wrote back.

Comic Book Superhero

You know when a guy looks so good on paper you can't imagine anything going wrong? That's what happened when I ran across the man I call Comic Book Superhero's profile on the site I have come to call "NOT OkCupid!"

Not only was CBS (not the TV network, the guy!) an extremely talented cartoon artist, on the phone he sounded like a true gentleman. I was incredibly excited to have piqued this obvious winner's interest, and started imagining myself at nerdy-yet-cool comic book conventions and glitzy movie premieres.

Our first meeting was promising. He had a cool rock and roll vibe. But while I generally love rockers—and CBS was not only successful, but a really nice guy—after a couple of dates I realized the chemistry just wasn't there. We agreed to be just friends.

End of story? Not by a long shot.

As we were now friends, I invited him to a party I was throwing with my former roommate Gwen. He showed up and seemed to forget the whole "just friends" thing—he was all over me like white on rice. I held firm, and finally he backed off and excused himself to head to the bathroom.

Where he remained for at least 45 minutes.

Relieved as I was to have him out of my hair, I started to worry. Did he fall in the toilet and drown? Was he ill? Did he pass out? I really just wanted him out of the apartment so I could go to bed. Everyone else was gone, but CBS remained, locked in the loo.

Finally, I put my ear up to the door, but all I heard was a squishing sound.

Bad vibe.

I peeked through the keyhole, and was met with the sight of soapsuds flying everywhere as the guy frenetically washed his hands, obviously over and over. Turns out CBS had a touch of OCD! Would he ever stop scrubbing and exit the premises? Or would I have to call 9-1-1 to break down the bathroom door?

Luckily, he ultimately exited the bathroom on his own, at which point he presented me with a small piece of artwork he had apparently created IN THE BATHROOM!

I still have the 2x2 picture: a rose. I guess he comes to parties prepared with a small square of paper and a pen.

I just hope he brings his own soap.

Anger Management

Lest you think OkCupid is the only dating website populated by the certifiably insane, I should probably warn you that Match.com is also home to a wide assortment of crazies. The guy I now call Anger Management is a prime example.

To be honest, I never should have agreed to a date with AM in the first place. He was from Weehawken, New Jersey, which is even more "outer borough" than the outer boroughs! However, like many of the expert self-promoters I've found on dating sites, he looked amazing on paper. He was tall, great looking, an athlete (he played hockey, which maybe should have offered a clue to his somewhat aggressive personality), and had a nice, stable job at a bank. Who wouldn't bend the rules for a catch like that?

Not only did I bend the rules for AM, we actually made it to the elusive fifth date. We reached this milestone despite the fact that those red flags were waving long before the incident that earned him his nickname. Basically, he seemed to have a bit of a temper. An edge. A weird vibe that indicated he might blow at any moment.

But he didn't. Until that fifth date.

He took me to his favorite restaurant, a "quaint" (and I use that term very generously) cafeteria-style barbecue place with karaoke in Chelsea.

Great—more karaoke! What's up with these guys and karaoke? I wondered if KS might make an appearance.

We each received a ticket, and then proceeded like high school students with trays in hand along the counter, where we selected our food from a variety of cafeteria-style delights. Then the server punched our tickets.

Classy, no?

Problem was, I'm not a big meat eater and all of the entrees looked like they could practically walk or fly out of the place. I opted for a green bean casserole and some other item that had a faint resemblance to a vegetable instead.

Despite the menu, we wound up having a blast joking and laughing for hours and making fun of the terrible karaoke singers that provided our entertainment. The chemistry between us was electric to the point that a woman at a neighboring table commented that we were either on a first date or madly in love.

Finally, it was time to end the cafeteria festivities and move on. That meant providing the checkout girl with our individual meal tickets so we could check out.

Here's where things started to head in a distinctly southerly direction. AM's ticket came in at a reasonable $40, while mine somehow totaled a whopping $120. Those were some pricey green beans, I guess.

Now, as you already know (remember Insufficient

Funds?), I always offer to split the check with my dates, but AM was too gentlemanly to allow this. On our previous dates, we followed his suggestion that I pay for the drinks and he pay for the food. However, because our entire bill was on these "tickets," and mine was so much higher than his was, I suggested that this time we split the bill 50/50.

He did not seem to like this suggestion. His entire demeanor changed. Meanwhile, I had no cash on me and tried to play the adorable damsel in distress by plopping a five-dollar bill—all the money I had—into the tip jar.

AM was not amused. As the line behind us grew, he violently slapped his credit card on the register and stormed out of the restaurant.

I ran after him, only to be greeted with a temper tantrum that seemed more appropriate for someone in his terrible twos. My mind was racing. Was he bipolar? Did he have multiple personality disorder? Is this how it all started with Ted Bundy?

He screamed like a man possessed, right there on the street, ranting and raving about how he had taken me out to dinner three times and I had never even offered to pay. This, of course, was wrong, meaning he was completely delusional. More importantly, he was terrifying. He was a full foot taller than me and was screaming as if he was about to cut my throat right there in front of all of Chelsea.

I started to plan the quickest possible escape from what felt like certain doom. He kept yelling, moving on to the fact that I was "expensive" and "high maintenance." Then, mercifully, he left me on the corner, but only after his unforgettable parting words: "This is why you are beautiful, almost thirty, and ALONE!"

I guess I couldn't have expected him to put me in a cab to make sure I got home safely given how "high maintenance" I am. I couldn't fathom what had just happened. Then I remembered he was from Jersey. What was my rule about dating guys from the "outer limits"? I made that rule for a reason: because they're WEIRD!

I headed to the subway, a little dazed and confused, but also relieved that the whole ugly scene was behind me. I bummed a cigarette from a guy standing outside the train to calm my nerves and wound up telling him the whole story of my verbal assault and almost battery at the hands of an unhinged giant from Jersey.

As if to prove chivalry isn't entirely dead, cigarette guy invited me to his party! Instead of going home and crying in my vodka and soda (again), I met a great guy, went to a party, and had a blast.

What's the moral of this story? For me, it is to squash that part of me that wants to give guys (that appear good on paper and have the pictures to match) the benefit of the doubt, and to take heed to red flags early on.

After all, they say Ted Bundy was hot, too.

Neighbor Ross

Part of the reason for my "no outer boroughs" dating rule may be the fact that, once upon a time, I actually lived in the outer boroughs. Forest Hills, Queens, to be specific. So I got to know the special charms of its residents firsthand.

Neighbor Ross was one of those borough boys. This would not turn out to be like a happy, wholesome episode of *Friends*, however.

NR lived in the apartment right next door to my step-sister. He asked her out, and like any sensible person, she shot him down. So he went after the next best option: me. And because I was young, fresh from my divorce, and hadn't set the potential suitor bar very high back then, and NR was good looking, gainfully employed, and had a place of his own, he passed muster.

Well, at least he passed mine.

Our first date was fine, and pleasant enough for me to agree to a second. At which point, things very quickly started to go south. Although those red flags were waving right in my face, it took a while for me to notice.

The first red flag appeared a mere three days after we met. He called me from the emergency room, begging me to meet him there because he had broken his nose playing basketball. Never one to turn down a man in need, I went, and soon learned that I had made a very big mistake. Almost instantly, he kicked our brand-new "relationship" up several notches, calling and texting me incessantly and referring to me as his "girl."

As I was now his "girl," I did the supportive thing and went to his soccer game on Randall's Island shortly thereafter. Mistake number two. Apparently, NR wanted to impress me by scoring a goal "for me." As he prepared to attempt this demonstration of combined athleticism and devotion, he glanced at me to make sure I was watching. Unfortunately, my eyes were not glued to my "man" at what he imagined would be his moment of glory. I was texting someone.

Well, apparently the sight of me *not* watching him was too much for poor NR. He missed the goal, his team lost, and he stormed past me in a full-on rage, convinced that they lost the game *because of me.* Yes, it turned out the outcome of an entire soccer game rested solely on the shoulders of someone who wasn't even on the field. Who knew I was that powerful?

Still, despite having witnessed this rather disturbing incident, I went back for more. I couldn't resist the lure of a good-looking guy who had a job and his own apartment and was clearly into me. So what if he happened to be certifiably insane? Nobody's perfect!

Later that week, I experienced a personal tragedy. Or at least a mini-tragedy. My beloved pet parrot died right in my hands. I called NR in tears and told him what happened, and also mentioned that I'd be late to watch the boxing match we had planned to view at his apartment with another couple.

Suddenly, the man who had been semi-obsessed with me revealed his true colors. He didn't care about my parrot. He didn't care about my feelings. He didn't care about *me*— only the presence of "his girl" at his apartment.

He demanded that I stop crying and get my raggedy ass over to his place immediately. And—this is the sick part—I actually did it! When I arrived, he put his arms tightly—VERY tightly—around me, in a way that was not intended to convey affection, but possession. To further drive the point home, he wouldn't even let me make my own drinks.

At this point, I realized something was not right. I was afraid of him.

Of course, just because I'm scared doesn't mean I'm a wimp. After his friends left, I confronted him about the way he was treating me and told him I didn't like it. I tried to leave, but he wouldn't let me. I was actually starting to fear for my life.

Then, in a 180-degree emotional turnaround, he started blubbering like a baby, sat me down on the couch, and told me that all he ever wanted to do was make his dad happy by scoring on the soccer field.

He insisted I accompany him to visit his dad. At the grave.

Yes, he wanted me to go with him to visit his dead father. What could possibly follow that but his dead mother—stuffed, dressed, and sitting in a rocking chair by the window upstairs?

I was finally able to escape and immediately severed all ties with him. Well, I tried to. He wasn't going to let me go so easily, and stated as much in the forty or so text messages and countless phone messages he left me the next day.

I stuck to my guns, and eventually, he stopped. Maybe he found another "girl" to obsess about. Or maybe the nice people from the mental hospital finally tracked down their escaped patient and returned him to the safety of his padded cell.

For which I will be eternally grateful.

Pathological Liar

Mr. Mythomania is another gem that I didn't meet on an online dating site—instead, our eyes met across a crowded bar at my friend Rose's birthday party. At first, I thought he was with a girl because a hot mess in a tight dress was very determinedly chatting him up. So, when he walked away and started talking to me, well, I felt like the luckiest girl in the room.

Which, you will soon learn, I was SO not.

PL told me he worked for LVMH as a high-powered

sales exec, which immediately appealed—what New York girl wouldn't give her left arm for a discount on a Louis Vuitton bag? Given his self-professed lofty perch in the fashion world, I wasn't surprised that our conversation mostly revolved around his elaborate stories of the posh parties and events he was constantly attending. When he suggested that I might accompany him to some of these events, I just about swooned. My job doesn't offer such swanky perks.

Except, for some reason, he always seemed to come up with some last-minute excuse as to why we couldn't go.

Turns out less-than-full disclosure was pretty much PL's standard operational procedure. No doubt, the nickname Pathological Liar was a dead giveaway. I, unfortunately, had to figure this out on my own.

One clue was the modest apartment he called home located in Red Hook, Brooklyn. Awesome! I rode the Ikea ferry across the river to visit him because the trains there suck. PL claimed that Kim Kardashian and Kris Humphries lived in the same building, swearing that he regularly saw Kim's ass waddling through the lobby as she headed to the gym. Granted, the building was passable—some might even call it nice—but I sincerely doubted any celebs would call it home.

Eventually, PL lured me to Atlantic City for a weekend, promising to hit up all of the hot spots including a Russian vodka place where you wear big fur coats and take shots inside a giant freezer. I was flattered—clearly, he listened to me when I said I love nothing more than a good vodka martini.

Unfortunately, the only thing that turned icy was my mood.

At some point during the weekend, we were going to

have to eat. We went out to dinner, during which he told me he paid someone $850 to have his taxes done. Moments later, his credit card was declined.

What were the odds?

I began to feel like Alice in Wonderland as things got curiouser and curiouser. I did a little Google stalking and found his LinkedIn profile—and was relieved to learn he actually did work for LVMH. However, his employment history was a little dicey: six months at one job, three months at another, and on and on.

Still, when he invited me to the very cool Veuve Clicquot boozy brunch at the Gansevoort Park Hotel, I decided to give him one last chance. Finally, he was going to take me to one of those glamorous fashion events he always talked about! He swore up and down that we were definitely going—to the point that I even bought a new dress for the occasion. I was so excited to finally rub couture-clad shoulders with all of his high rolling colleagues.

You can probably guess how this story ends.

The night before the big event, I received a text message from PL informing me that he had pulled a ligament at the gym. Nothing more, nothing less. So, I held out hope. He didn't cancel! I bought a dress! He promised!

The next day, I watched anxiously as the hours passed. Two hours before the brunch was slated to start, I called him.

No answer.

So I texted him.

ME: Hey how r u feeling?

ME: We still on for today?

PL: *So I know what I have...A broken ligament on my wrist and possibly some hyper-extended tendons ....FML*

ME: I'm really sorry u hurt your wrist. I get that stuff happens but did u plan on calling or texting me yesterday to tell me we weren't hanging out? I called u 2 hours before we were supposed to go to the "boozy" brunch event (I've heard about nothing but that for two weeks)... I even had a cute outfit picked out again....

I was so pissed off that I deleted his replies so I can't reprint them here. He basically wrote that he was in too much pain to go to the brunch, and had passed out on painkillers. He also accused me of not caring about him, or the fact that he was in pain, and I only gave a rat's ass about going to the brunch. And, because he needed someone to care for him in his weakened state, his Mommy and Daddy (did I mention he was thirty-three years old?) were coming over to lay out his clothes for the rest of the week and bring him food!

After learning all this, I sent him another message.

ME: Some things you've said just don't make sense to me and it's been on my mind since before this. Your stories don't match up. I'm pretty good at reading people so just be honest with me. We have been out several times and u continue to tell me about these amazing events, but they never materialize.

Please don't pump everything up if it's not going

to happen. I honestly could care less about going but u continued to talk and talk and get me excited, just to be let down once again. I must admit it is a turn-off. And then Sunday rolls around and I don't hear from u all day. Something is very off here.

No response. So I wrote again.

ME: Hope you're feeling better. Sorry for blowing up. Maybe I'm just not ready to be serious with anyone yet.

PL: I'm feeling better. Thanks for asking. Apology accept-ed and I promise it won't happen again. How was your day? I have been in back to back meetings!!! Crazy crazy!

PL: I'm still at work :(I have to go upstate tomorrow till Friday but I want to plan something for you... :)

ME: I really don't think I'm ready to be serious with any-one. I have a lot going on...

PL: Was just asking to hangout not get serious but I'm getting your gist...

Oh well. We'll always have the Russian vodka bar—in my head. Oh yeah, we never did go there either!

What I've learned from my experiences with mixed nuts:
- We are all a little crazy. However, there's good, fun, wholesome crazy, like let's go jump in the lake at the Boat House. (My friend's boyfriend actually did this. Complete gross factor with all of the slime

and turtle and duck poop but it was pee your pants hysterical looking at the faces of the people paddle boating by.) Then there's you've got a chemical imbalance crazy as seen in the stories you just read. Know the difference.

- If you notice any red flags, pay attention! You don't want them to explode in your face later on.

Sixteen

Second-Hand Rose (Dating Divorced Men... Or Men Who Wish They Were)

Time for some full disclosure here: With the possible exception of James Bond, whose marital status was never exactly clear to me, I haven't had the pleasure of dating a lot of divorced guys.

I use the term "pleasure" rather loosely.

Dating a man who's been married before is a lot like buying a used car: They might look shiny and new on the outside, but they've been around the block and might be hiding some pretty serious damage.

A typical divorced guy in his thirties or forties is probably paying alimony and/or child support to his bitter ex-wife, who more than likely lives in their suburban house, probably in Westchester, with their kids. Meaning, he won't be able to see you on weekends, because that's when Mom sends the kids out the door for her weekly "me time."

When the kids aren't around, guys who are freshly divorced (or who are going through one), depending on their age, almost automatically revert to their post-college lifestyle. They typically end up moving back into the city loaded down with Ikea furniture, where they consume copious amounts of pizza and beer.

Of course, with more than half of all marriages ending in a court of law, divorced guys do make up a large portion of the fish in the dating pool. I mean, even I'm divorced—I just forget sometimes because it seems like another lifetime.

So if you're going to settle for a second-hand rose, it's best to be aware of the accompanying thorns. The best way to do that is by asking a few—okay, more than a few—prescient questions.

- Was the divorce cheating related—and if so, who was the cheater?

- Is he a drinker, a druggie, or a nutcase? Is she?

- Did God (or Allah or Buddha or Satan) come between him and his ex?

- Were there problems in the sack?

- Is he out on parole for killing her?

- Who dumped whom?

- Are there rugrats involved…and where do those rugrats reside?

- Who pays for the kids' preschool and the ex-wife's visits to Saks?

- Can he afford to pay for his kids' preschool and his ex's trips to Saks and still have enough left to take care of you?

- Does he bash his ex? Does he cry about her?

- How long since the marriage blew up?

- Did he see a marriage counselor, or his nearest bartender?

- Does he actually want a relationship, or just some "no strings" sex?

- Is he over his marriage, or is he still nursing a raw wound?

According to the experts, you don't want to get involved with a divorced guy until at least a year after his marriage ended (the aforementioned "healing period") and you don't want to be his first relationship (known as the "rebound" or "transitional relationship"). Leave all that to some other, less savvy girl.

That said, a divorced guy doesn't have to be "damaged goods"; many men actually do manage to learn something from their divorces and use that knowledge to have happier, healthier post-divorce relationships. Okay, not many, but definitely some of them. Plus, on the upside, divorced men:

- Have proven that they can live with a woman.

- May have even proven they want kids. Whether or not they want more kids is the question.

Besides, just because one relationship crashed and burned doesn't mean their next one will. We are all human, wanting someone to love and for someone to love us back.

However, this doesn't mean you're out of the woods

because, as the old saying goes, it takes two to tango. Which means if a relationship with a divorced guy is going to work, you also need to ask yourself a few questions, including:

- Are you actually compatible—or is it just that excitement of meeting a guy who doesn't make you want to throw up?

- Does he want the same things out of life that you do?

- Do you mind sharing him with kids, especially kids who might have a problem with Dad's new girlfriend?

- Do you want kids of your own—and is he up for more?

- Do you already have kids—and do they like this guy at least half as much as you do?

If the answers to most of the questions in this chapter are positive, you may have a shot at a healthy, happy relationship with a man who has learned a lot about himself and what he wants in a woman. So, go ahead and go for it...as long as you proceed with caution.

However, do everything in your power to avoid men who are newly separated, going through a divorce, or have yet to grow the balls required to ask for a permanent parting of ways. You may not automatically recognize these sloppy seconds because they're the guys who hide their wedding rings by strategically placing their left hand in their pocket for the entire duration of happy hour.

Or they just leave the ring at home.

More on that in the next chapter.

Seventeen

The M-Bomb

Dating a divorced guy, or even an "officially separated" guy, is one thing. Dating a married man is something else entirely. Because, nine times out of ten, you aren't actually made aware of the fact that the man you're buying that hot new dress to impress has a wife—no doubt with a closet full of dresses herself—back home.

On one level, I get it. I really do. I was married once. I know that special flavor of misery that only a bad marriage can produce: A bitter mix of loneliness and regret with the spicy tang of horniness that comes from not having sex for months on end.

Are any married people actually happy? I know some who are, including friends of mine who were lucky enough to find their ideal match. But I have met so many guys in their late thirties who wish they didn't marry so young, didn't have that family and move to the suburbs, and took some time to grow up and figure out who they really were before they promised to spend the rest of their lives with another person.

Then there are those other married men.

There are men who have no shame and will boldly tell you they're married, then ask you out on a date! Oh, they'll have some excuses ready to go: Maybe their wife cheats, too; maybe they're in a loveless/open marriage; maybe they're staying in it for the children; maybe they're in the process of getting separated… There is an endless number of perfectly plausible justifications for why it's totally normal for them to be married and ask you out.

And you have only one perfectly plausible answer: NO!

Of course, that doesn't help with the scumbags who don't even bother to tell you in the first place.

Miles

After running another marathon in Arizona, my teammate and I decided we desperately needed some down time and headed to Vegas for some sun and sin. There I learned how truly small this world is—there, at the poker table at Caesar's Palace, was one of my ex's work colleagues, Miles.

Miles was actually there with Burak, but luckily, God decided not to punish me that night and allowed Burak to get so pathetically drunk that he had to leave the party early.

Leaving Miles with nothing more exciting to do than entertain me.

Ever the gentleman, Miles funded my efforts at the poker table, where our fellow gamblers included a bald guy from Texas, his sugar mama, and a twenty-one-year-old college kid. His gallantry evaporated, however, when I made a quick trip to the rest room, during which Miles shared enough information about me to fill an entire segment of *Biography*. They knew about my marriage to Burak, our divorce, and even how Burak married someone else in record time after we split up.

I was not amused.

Nevertheless, Miles was dropping a lot of money on that poker table on my behalf. Playing with someone else's cash is so much more enjoyable than playing with your own, especially when the cocktails are also free.

After quite a few of those cocktails, Miles actually convinced me to go up to Burak's room to say "hi" to my ex. Amazingly, I went, but luckily, he was so drunk that he was totally incoherent, and would probably have no memory of seeing me. That mission accomplished, Miles and I opted to blow that Popsicle stand and move on to greener pastures at a hot club at the Luxor.

The last thing I remember was partying until the wee hours of the morning.

Then I woke up—in the hotel room of my ex-husband's business associate. His very married business associate, whose wife is an absolute doll. Whoopsie!

All I could think was OMG what have I done? Did he roofie me? Did I just black out? What the hell??

Well, since I don't actually remember what took place, I decided that there was no hanky-panky involved. We just passed out.

What? It's possible!

If we did, in fact, hook up, then it doesn't count because everyone knows what happens in Vegas stays in Vegas.

Needless to say, we made a pact to never breathe a word of what happened that night. But here's the kicker:

Two weeks later, coincidently, I received a text message from Miles' wife asking me how I was doing.

I didn't tell her I might have been doing her husband.

St. Paddy's Day Cop

I've already shared some of my St. Patrick's Day adventures in this book, so you should now have some awareness of what happens to New York—and specifically New York's Finest—every March 17. However, the man I have nicknamed St. Paddy's Day Cop has earned a special place in my dating pantheon because he managed to outdo all the other St. Paddy's slimeballs and leave them in the dust.

The scene of this particular crime was a huge St. Patrick's Day blow out at Pier 42—an annual event that I believe is held for the sole purpose of getting our boys in blue as sloppy drunk as possible. Of course, I wasn't exactly sober myself. Which must be why, after a night of alcohol-fueled flirting, I allowed an off-duty police officer to escort me in a cab back to my apartment—where we totally hooked up.

Well, no harm done. It's not as if he was wearing a wedding ring or anything.

Except the next day, the friend who introduced us texted me to ask if I knew what happened to our police officer pal. Because his wife, who was home alone with their one-month-old newborn baby, was frantic that he never came home!

My bad.

After berating myself for a good fifteen minutes, I coolly responded to my friend and told her that the last time I saw cop man he was headed to the Metro-North to take the train home.

Needless to say, I didn't mention where he was heading home *from*.

I felt horrible. But my new friend? Not so much. In fact, he sent me about a zillion texts asking if he could come back for a repeat performance!

When I finally answered, I told him:

A) that I knew he was married and had a child, and,

B) he was, therefore, a total scumbag.

His reply? "If it means anything, I think you're a great girl."

It doesn't. But yes, I am.

Pigalle

By now, you are no doubt well aware of my weakness for foreign men. Therefore, it should come as no surprise that Pigalle, who is French, educated, *and* a journalist covering foreign affairs swept me off my feet when I met him (in person!) in the city.

It felt amazing having this powerful, worldly, and (I thought at the time) "mature" man by my side. And, even though he was ridiculously well traveled and sophisticated, he still came across as sweet and innocent.

When I asked him when his last relationship had ended, he replied that it had been a whole year ago, that he had no children because he traveled so much, and that it was difficult to find a woman who would be in it for the long haul. Score for Mary, I thought. I began conjuring up pictures in my head of us skiing the French Alps and drinking hot toddies by the fireplace.

This is a chapter on married men, however.

We saw each other a handful of times, always at the

most exclusive restaurants and bars thanks to his glamorous job. I was so smitten and so convinced he was a nice guy that I even broke the Lip Slut rule and spent the night (yes, in the biblical sense) in his hotel room. Hey, who doesn't love hotel sex?

After what would turn out to be our final visit, I sent him the following gushy email, which began the exchange that would put an end to everything. Pay special attention to the climax—it's a shocker!

ME: If the Mayan calendar is correct and the world should end tomorrow, I just want to let you know that I had such a great time with you the other night and I'm happy we met! =o)

   PS – What is your address?

PIG: *I can't tell you how this evening was so great for me! I miss your kiss so much now. Just arrived tonight to my parents place for a couple of days for X-mas. I will probably go to beach tomorrow to enjoy walk.*

   Why my address? Do you want to send me your book? :) No way, I expect to come soon in NY and get a dedicated one :)

   Je t'embrasse

In case you're wondering, this was a more recent encounter. But I'm learning, I swear…

PIG: *I wish you a magnificent birthday, my dear! I miss you already. Just back from X-mas at my parents' place. Yeah, it is just a couple of miles from the beach and it is* *always great to come back to walk on the sand. Now I am preparing to go skiing with friends for two days.*

ME: Thanks! Merry Christmas to you and your family from Valentino and yours truly. I was simply asking for your address so I could send you a holiday card, but it's no big deal because by the time it would get there it would be January already. So, your parents live by a beach? Nice! I hope you're enjoying some time off.

Xo

I sent a second email after not hearing back from him for a couple of weeks. Unusual, I thought, considering we had been emailing each other about five times a day since we met.

ME: How are you? You must be real busy! Just wanted to say hello and I hope you had a fantastic New Year's. So much has changed in the past few weeks but I won't bore you with everything. When are you back in NYC?

ME: You vanished on me! Is everything okay? I'm sure you are busy, but if you have started dating someone or met a girlfriend and no longer wish to talk, then it's okay. Just let me know and I wish you all the best. But I really did enjoy hanging out with you and emailing.

Eventually, I did get a response. But not from Pigalle...

Dear Mary,

You are probably not aware of the fact that I am

[Pigalle's] wife and that we also have two children togeth-er, aged three and five. The 'friends' he went skiing with during Christmas Holidays was actually me, his wife.

Please accept his apologies for not telling you the truth and for not answering you lately, as he also has a busy family life. I am glad to hear that you enjoy hanging out with him and dating him. I just hope it won't happen again.

Thanks again for your comprehension.

Honestly, you can't beat the French when it comes to mas-tering the art of the sophisticated understatement.

Oh, in case you're still wondering where Pigalle's nickname came from, Pigalle was a raunchy neighborhood in Paris during WWII. Plus, Pigalle sounds a lot like pig, which is what dear Pigalle turned out to be.

So...what have the married men taught me?

- One thing and one thing only: STAY AWAY!

Eighteen
The Party's Over, or,
Knowing When to Say Goodbye

At this point, it's no secret that I've experienced just about every form of dating disaster known to man. Or woman.

I've spent time with enough crazies, liars, bad dressers, losers, mama's boys, moochers, and other assorted weirdoes to fill a book. Which, coincidentally, I have!

But the thing is, when you get right down to it, this veritable encyclopedia's worth of dates were also experiences that have all helped shape me in some way. Life is a journey, and our experiences help fill our book. Good or bad, each one of my "nicknames" has helped me figure out what I want (and what I don't want!) in a life partner. They've helped me grow into a more mature, self-aware woman, and in the end, while I still drive myself crazy sometimes asking "Why doesn't he like me?" "Why did he disappear?" and my personal favorite, "Why was he so fuckin' weird?" most of those guys never really mattered all that much. A lot of them were good for a laugh, or at least a great story to entertain my girlfriends later. When it was over, after I licked my wounds, it was still pretty easy to move on. In fact, most of the time I moved on before things even got started!

The ones that stick with me are the ones that don't make it so easy.

In almost every single girl's life, there's one (or more) of those relationships that you just can't walk away from. A relationship where everything seems right—even feels right—and you put everything you have into it. Then, all of a sudden, you just get stuck. Eventually, you realize you have to say goodbye.

Sebastian

Sebastian is the only guy in this book besides Giorgio in Chapter 3 who doesn't get a nickname. Even though he and I didn't end up living happily ever after, he'll always be special to me. Therefore, in real life, I use the name his parents gave him—although his real name was changed for the purpose of this book.

Sebastian found me on How About We. He sent me an email. When I saw he was tall, dark, handsome, and Latino (of course), I was more than happy to meet him. In person, he was super intelligent and eloquent. To be honest, he was a little nerdy, which for me is a major turn on. Hot and nerdy: Score again, I thought at the time! I fell hard for this one.

He was also *amazing* in bed. We even went to a sex shop in our third month of dating—my first visit ever (much to my besties' surprise). I may be the only single woman in her thirties who has never owned a vibrator. Well, until that fateful date, anyway.

Unfortunately, outside the sheets, Sebastian was not quite as much fun.

To be honest, he was somewhat boring, like watching paint dry. Mainly because he worked fourteen-hour days as an executive and spent the other ten hours feeling totally stressed out about his job. Instead of partying and letting loose to relieve some of that stress, when we went out he refused to have more than one drink and spent most of the time crying about work.

Yeah, he was kind of a Debbie Downer. But hey, at least I sobered up! I even lost six pounds.

Besides, a man who is responsible and professional is a good thing, right? Especially when the sex is amazing. So I stayed with Sebastian and I did everything I could to make it work. You've probably noticed I like my dates to take me out on the town and show me a good time. I want a partner in crime. Why do you think I live in NYC—for the low rent and clean streets? But I had no problem going to Sebastian's place on a Friday or Saturday night and doing absolutely NOTHING because I really, really liked him. I even made him my famous stuffed chicken with sundried tomatoes, artichokes, and fontina cheese along with my equally famous Martha Stewart garlic roasted mashed potatoes!

I don't do that for any old guy.

My efforts seemed to be working. Sebastian was the first guy in six years that I dated for more than three months. We saw each other exclusively and talked every day. I even took him to my boss's wedding. He certainly treated me like his girlfriend.

He just wouldn't *call* me his girlfriend.

Even after four months of seeing each other constantly, he said he didn't want a "title." He had friends who went down the slippery cheating slope—crimes Sebastian would never want to commit himself—so he refused to commit to me.

Plus, he was so stressed from working sixty to seventy hours a week he told me he was seriously considering quitting his job and moving to India. He offered to try to work through this rough patch with me, provided I was willing to wait it out and could promise I wouldn't get upset if he suddenly decided to pack up and move across the earth.

In his defense, he told me he should probably be in therapy. Unfortunately, he didn't go.

I called bullshit. I told him whether he's with me or another girl, he can't live his entire life running away from commitment. What was the point, anyway? It was painfully obvious we both weren't seeing anyone else.

But Sebastian wouldn't budge. Without knowing what I meant to him, or if our relationship was going anywhere, I couldn't help feeling as though I was wasting my time.

Eventually, instead of talking every day, our contact dwindled down to text messages every two or three days. I didn't want to accept it, but our relationship was obviously fizzling out.

Then came the email:

Hi Mary,

Hope all is going well. Apologies that it took me so long to get back to you.

I wanted to take a minute to apologize for how things ended between us. Things unfortunately are not going the way I would have liked during the past few months as my job has pretty much taken over my life and right now has created a major imbalance, to the point that it's affecting my health. Anyhow, I'm not writing to complain as I have already done enough of that. I've felt terrible during the past few weeks about the way I abruptly disappeared and wanted to apologize for being this rude. Its very unlike me and in looking back many of the things I'm doing right now are unlike me, which is not a good sign. I've been doing some soul searching during the past few weeks and hope to make major changes. In fact, I recently met with a friend and she couldn't believe how much had changed with me in such a short period of time (that was a wake up call). Whatever those changes will be, they are meant to happen. Life is too short for us not to be doing the things we are passionate about.

I really enjoyed every minute I spend with you and Val and didn't want you to be part of all this negativity going on in my life right now. You are one of the most positive people I've met and considering all you have gone through, this is the last thing you needed. My intention was never to waste your time and my sincere apologies if you feel that way. You didn't deserve this!

Anyhow, I really hope you are thrilled about your upcoming trip to Australia and about all the great experiences that await you. I have no doubt that you'll have an amazing time out there and all those diving lesson will make it all worthwhile. I hope to soon have an extended vacation to sort things out.

I miss you and Val.
Say hi to the little angel.

Two days later, I received an alert on my HAW app that new dates were posted in my area. I clicked on it and there, staring me in the face, was Sebastian, along with his proposed date: "How about we go have a picnic in Central Park?"

Just waiting for an unsuspecting woman looking for love to accept his invitation, like I did a few months before.

Two weeks later, I learned that his post was successful—not only was he exchanging emails with a new woman, but that woman was one of my good friends! Luckily, once I filled her in on who Sebastian was, she, being a good friend, immediately ceased communication with him

I, however, had to admit to myself that it was time to move on. I had met a Turkish guy—well, Turkish, but born in the United States. (The Turks have a way of sniffing me out if you haven't figured this out by now.) On the train out to Montauk, we talked nonstop for the entire three-hour trip, so clearly there was some kind of connection. But I was still hoping Sebastian and I were going to go the distance, so even though I gave the Turk my number I kept blowing off his texts asking me for a date.

Plus, he lived in Queens.

However, as it started to become clearer and clearer that Sebastian and I were not destined to live happily ever after, I decided it was time to break my Borough Boy rule. I invited my new friend from Queens to meet me for drinks at a bar in my neighborhood.

It was a typical outer borough first date. He was forty minutes late getting into the city and finding parking. His shirt matched the wallpaper in the bathroom—a fact he proudly pointed out to me. There were no fireworks.

He was a really nice guy; he kept complimenting me

all night on my clothes, the bar, pretty much everything about the evening. But that was kind of the problem.

Manhattan was like some magical fairyland to him.

We were definitely not compatible.

I realized he might not agree with that assessment. He kept trying to kiss me all night long, and when he was nice enough to walk me home, I had to relent and give him a peck.

But after Sebastian, a guy in his mid thirties who lives with four roommates in an apartment in Queens—no matter how nice he is—just wasn't going to cut it.

I'm hoping my next date will. Or maybe the one after that.

Nineteen

Where Do I Go From Here?

I've learned a lot from my years on the singles scene. Basically, dating is a numbers game. The more men you meet, the greater your chances of meeting the right one and adding a few nicknames under your belt along the way. However, I've also learned that there is no such thing as the perfect guy. Love doesn't always come easily, and even if it seems like it does with all of the hormones jumping around your body, shit happens.

All I can do is just be myself and keep on keepin' on having fun in this fabulous, crazy city. Whatever is going on in my love life (or lack thereof), life is good. I'll remain optimistic and positive whether I'm flying solo or have a beau. In the meantime, I'll continue to get companionship from other sources: my friends, pets, and the occasional booty call.

I still hope that one day I will finally meet my partner in crime. I think I'll know I've met a keeper when I don't have to examine the relationship and when I call him by his real name. Until then, I won't settle (and neither should you) just to have a snuggle buddy on Sunday nights.

If I'm forty and still flying solo, maybe I'll freeze my eggs or something (or find a gay best friend to knock me up—joking!).

Of course, there's always my dog. He doesn't talk back and he's always happy to see me regardless of my outfit. Also, my dog doesn't bring condoms to dinner or care how my morning breath smells.

My final words: Trust your instinct and be prepared for big bumps in the road.

CPSIA information can be obtained at www.ICGtesting.com
Printed in the USA
BVOW06s0238021015

420713BV00010B/46/P